DEAR TILLY

Dear
Tilly

by LILLIAN MANNOOCH

EGON PUBLISHERS LTD
Meeting House Lane, Church Street,
Baldock, Herts. SG7 5BP

First published in 1981
by Egon Publishers Ltd.
Meeting House Lane, Church Street, Baldock, Herts.

Copyright © Egon Publishers Ltd.
and Lillian Mannooch

ISBN 0 905858 16 6

Illustrations by Roy Mitchell
Bookjacket design by Joan Matthews

Printed in England by
S. G. Street & Co. Ltd
Meeting House Lane, Church Street,
Baldock, Herts. SG7 5BP

DEDICATION

This book is written in gratitude to my dear husband, James, Mrs Tilly Tomlins, a wonderful neighbour, and two good friends, Peggy and Nobby.

FOREWORD

THIS book is an accurate account of the running of a stately home registered for 21 guests from 1965 until 1972, though names have been changed so that embarrassment will not be caused to relatives.

The story is told in the form of letters to a dear friend, Tilly Tomlins, of how I came to "Ash Court", and what I found when I got there.

The joys, the worries, the headaches, the humorous situations have all been included, together with a few of the funny and sometimes precognitive dreams, of which I have (privately) recorded an average of between four and five hundred each year.

Throughout the country there are many owners of homes who probably run their establishments better than we have done, but I can only claim to have done my best, and to have enjoyed deep, loving relationships.

I hope also that this book may prevent people from buying homes on borrowed money unless they are fully aware of the need for total commitment.

At the time of writing I am living in a modern house with three guests, one of whom is 97 years of age and has been with me for 15 years. Since leaving "Ash Court" we have had a further 11 eventful but happy years without even a day off, and we've enjoyed these years.

I hope, dear reader, that you will share with me and enjoy this fascinating insight into the real-life drama of "Ash Court".

Lillian Mannooch

Dear Tilly,

Before I tell you the news I must tell you about the three silly dreams I recorded last night.

At 2.45 am I dreamt I was in Moscow at the Kremlin, instructing Brezhnev on the way to run old people's homes! (Note the "instructing" bit!). I said we would need a lot of accountants.

"What do you mean, accountants?" thundered Brezhnev, and I explained.

"What? You waste money paying men to count? We have our own accountnuts. They count with their nuts!" he roared, pointing to a row of squirrels on a window sill, who were all picking up nuts rapidly.

The next minute I was walking quietly through the streets in the dark, inspecting locks on the doors of Marks and Spencers and Woolworths. The Government said someone was fiddling the electricity from them, so I had to pay the electricity bill for all Britain!

At 6.10 am I dreamt I opened the fridge door and a small milkman with a peaked cap and a blue and white striped butcher's apron over a white coat, handed me a carton. I shut the door, opened it again, and said, "I have my milk in bottles!" He handed me bottles of milk and then I took a beautiful iced sponge cake from a young girl and placed it in the fridge.

At 7 am I dreamt I saw an eight foot tall green Yeti in the middle of the road. I was frightened and said, "I'm not passing that." A man said, "Don't be silly, it's the new council uniform." Turning round I saw another Yeti carrying a can of paint. His shoes were protruding from his bright green fur. I next walked into Barclays Bank where they were selling shoes for £250,000 a pair and the manager complained that people kept stealing them.

"Well, they would at that price. I'll lend you my private detective," I told him.

The second dream has partly come true. I was presented with a beautiful iced sponge at noon and the milkman, who always comes to the door, came to the window for the first time and, passing through a carton said, "Here's a free sample for you."

I can laugh now, but I was cross with myself this week. I bought the most expensive pair of tights and, putting them on the next morning, noticed a flaw running up my leg.

"This is dreadful after spending so much money. I'll take them back this morning," I said. Two hours later, was my face red when the pleasant assistant held them up to the light and said, "They're seamed tights. You put them on back to front, madam!"

There is always something humorous to raise one's spirits. This week I made everyone laugh when I told your story about your brother on his first date 60 years ago, when he sneaked upstairs and borrowed your father's new coat, knowing he could put it back before your father finished work, hoping it would make a good impression on the young lady. Sitting in the dark in the cinema, he placed a bag of sweets in her hand, whereupon she squealed, slapped him around the face — and fled. I explained that he'd been unaware that your father had been fitted with new teeth, and had bought some hard boiled sweets on the way home. He had popped one in his mouth hoping it would help him to get used to the teeth, but they were so uncomfortable he put the teeth back in the bag with the sweets. That was the end of the romance.

Now I shall explain all that has happened here. I arrived here at 4 pm last Monday and, after tea, was shown around this stately William and Mary mansion, set on the brow of a hill facing parkland. The hall is very gracious with two Corinthian pillars flanked on either side by handsome carved oak chests, each supporting a variety of colourful plants. Beyond the pillars the hall opens out, revealing three large double bay windows on the right hand side and a magnificent eight foot wide staircase on the left hand side. A grand piano, five settees draped in matching chintz covers, small tables, pot plants, and a double aquarium of tropical fish, create an impression of elegance, peace and comfort. A cloakroom and two large lounges lead directly off the hall, and a wide corridor led me to the dining room, another 50 foot lounge and the bathroom. Beyond this lies the domestic quarters which consist of a 40 by 30 foot kitchen and another half-a-dozen rooms.

I inspected the 14 bedrooms, most with private bathrooms. Some have views facing over the front drive, others over the back drive, but the main rooms overlook the sweeping lawn from which one has uninterrupted views over the parkland. Ash trees, huge oaks, lime trees, magnolias, and the weeping willow over the pond enhance the glorious view. A self-contained four-bedroomed flat, in which one guest and two staff live, leads off the main building. Above the second floor there is a small self-contained flat with access to the attics proper. The 21 elderly guests have their own rooms and seem to be very happy, each one greeting me warmly when I was introduced as a friend.

I spent the evening discussing the accounts with the owner. He is a retired naval officer who bought the goodwill, plus all the furniture and fittings, seven years before from the previous owner, who had bought the property three years before him and decided to run it as a rest home. He has had to meet the required fire safety standards and has installed fire escapes and smoke doors. He also installed an oil-fired central heating boiler, which means that the home is only now beginning to show a profit. Nobody pays cash and everything is above board.

I went to bed and decided I would abide by whatever decision the bank manager came to when I kept the appointment I had arranged with him for the next day. I thought about the staffing problems that the owner had described to me. The two outdoor staff are efficient and capable, but he has had a series of cooks and found it impossible to get British living-in staff. He has employed several Spanish staff and had to assure the authorities that he was employing them only because he couldn't get English staff. In each case the Spanish staff have left within six weeks, having merely used the situation to enable them to move on to another job in Britain. There is one woman working here who was a mental hospital patient, so, if I buy and I can't get reliable living-in staff I will make more use of that contact.

Tilly, I left the bank manager the next day prepared to forget the whole business, as he had said. "I'll lend you money to buy a freehold place, but not a leasehold place of that size. There are great changes ahead of us in this country and, more than likely, there is going to be high inflation throughout the world by the time the lease comes up for renewal. Supposing the rent is increased twenty- or even forty-fold, plus all the other increases you could face? Inflation will cause some businesses, industrial and otherwise, to fail. Many old people who have their savings invested in them will find they cannot afford to pay the fees of rest homes or nursing homes. I hope this situation won't arise but I'm afraid it very likely will. You look for a freehold business to buy and I shall help you."

I discussed this with Commander Mannooch that evening and, as I studied his gentle, kind face, I detected a great disappointment. He had already lost two potential buyers so I wondered if their bank managers had given them the same advice. He asked me if I would like to stay for the rest of the week and by the end of the week, a partnership had been mooted.

You will think I'm mad. Here am I, five feet nothing, red-haired and impulsive, considering taking on new headaches after the experiences of owning a restaurant for seven years, working as a trained nurse, hotel manageress, estimating order clerk, pools checker, and driver of a baker's horse and cart for two months. Instead of going into partnership I should be sitting down and writing about them all. However, the die is cast and eventually I'll sell the house — not without heartache, as I think of the happy times we had there.

The guests and staff seem to have accepted me and yesterday the

Commander and staff enjoyed a good laugh over the following episode. I was checking that the tables were correctly laid in the dining room when I overheard voices through the door leading into the lounge. A gentleman with a north country accent said, "Ee, I do like her."

"Who?" replied a lady named Mrs Lace.

"Her. You know, the new one."

Mrs Lace countered "I don't know who you mean."

"Yes you do," he replied, "her with the red hair; her that's big up 'ere." I rushed to the office to repeat this gem and, as I left the office a few minutes later, I met Mrs Lace who asked if I would go to her room. I agreed, but I don't know how I managed to keep a straight face when I thanked her as she handed me four pairs of the most enormous brassieres I've ever seen, saying, "I've been wanting to make a present of these to you. They'll keep you in."

I don't think life will be dull here. It never is when you're involved in doing things for other people. Yesterday, while having tea with the guests, I told them the story about when I bought a horse at Ashdown market having gone to buy some chickens. You remember, it nuzzled my shoulder and, looking at its gentle brown eyes, I made a fuss of it and said to the woman owner, "How much do you want for her?"

"Fifty pounds," she replied.

"Done!"

I told them how you stood beside me as the horse-box came rumbling down the unmade road through the orchard. Mr Blundell helped us unload the chickens and one laid an egg in his hand. We tethered the horse behind the chicken shed and when Roy came home I said, "I've got a surprise for you," and putting some bread in his hand led him to look at her.

"No! What have you done?" he said.

"You always said when we moved back to the country you'd buy me a pony," I said, adding, "she's beautiful."

"Never! What do you mean, she's beautiful? It's not a 'she' at all. It's a male, undoctored and unshod, and could be a danger to children passing by. It must go back tomorrow."

I then told them how, later that day, we drove into the hospital where I was due to commence duty on the surgical ward at 9 pm and repeated the story to a farmer's wife who used to come on duty two nights a week. She agreed to look after the horse, so I relaxed during my off-duty period, but when I returned to the ward the men were in fine form. I'd had the early break and they hadn't gone to sleep.

"Fancy not being able to tell the difference nurse, when you've seen so many!" said one. "You're always saying, 'Come now, put your rose in this vase here'." They continued to pull my leg about it for weeks.

12

Some of the guests had a good laugh, a few smiled and a few seemed as though they didn't know what I was talking about.

I wait for your letter with interest. Give my love to Phyllis, and little Sweet Pea. I can never think of her as Leslie, she has a face like a flower.

Much love,
Lillian.

3rd APRIL, 1965

Dear Tilly,

Thank you for all your news. I miss you all, although much has happened since I last wrote to you. The nice gentleman who liked "Her that's big up 'ere," unfortunately fell and struck his head on the floor and died. A lady booked his room and, oh dear, Tilly, I was horrified. She was tall, sweet-faced, dark-haired and of a most pleasant disposition, but when I went in to say goodnight as I always do between 10 pm and 10.30 pm, I found her standing in the centre of her room with a cigarette in her hand, two still alight smouldering in an ashtray, and another one on the floor.

I searched the drawers and luggage and removed the cigarettes and matches, but found it difficult to get to sleep. Jim (oh yes, we've got to the Christian name stage now) always inspects all the furniture in the lounge and hall at midnight in case a stray cigarette has worked its way down the side of an armchair. He told me that three times he's found one smouldering. (By the way, he's had five ceilings down as a result of guests washing their hands before lunch and absent-mindedly coming downstairs and leaving the plug in with both taps running!)

The following day I phoned the relatives, and they removed their mother when I explained that she needed to be where there were staff on night duty. We don't charge enough to be able to take guests who need monitoring every hour. I sat up all night with a guest who was ill the other night, which I don't mind, but obviously I couldn't keep anyone who needed to be nursed night after night.

A 91-year-old guest named Mrs Hart, an ex-suffragette, is a remarkable character. She holds cocktail parties every morning at 11.30 but three weeks ago she poured out too much gin, fell, and broke her femur. You won't believe this, but it's true. They brought her back with a Zimmer yesterday, and she flung it away and said, "I'm not using that damn thing! It will trip someone up. Hand me my stick." This morning I noticed she was feeling for her brushes on the dressing table, so we must make an appointment to get her eyes inspected.

We have a marvellous cook but she's terribly extravagant! She cooked a six-pound ham beautifully and carved it up to go with the salad on Sunday night. Later, I noticed it was nearly all in the chicken bowl as she'd cut it an inch thick! I praised her cooking but said it would be better if I carved the ham in future.

"Ah now, oi'll not be having that, for haven't the greatest chefs in the world told me oi'm the greatest carver they've met," said cheerful plump Miss O'Hara, who is in her middle 50's. Have you got any ideas how I can get over this problem?

The two outdoor staff, Rose and Jenny, are very good. Rose has worked for Jim from the beginning. Joan, who lives in, apparently suffered with her nerves. She left her husband and ended up in a mental hospital, from which she came to work here a couple of months before I arrived. She's tall, dark, well-spoken and quiet, and liked by all.

It's time to send letters round for an increase. We're asking another ten shillings per week. Two guests haven't got enough money to pay, but Jim has let them stay as they have lived here about six years, and haven't any relations. The increase will mean we can take another person on to the payroll to help out.

It's lovely to see the Spring flowers blooming. We all enjoy the garden. When the sun's out most of the guests are out, but with all the grandiose scenery it has not got the charm of the orchard, Tilly. I can see all the cherry, apple, pear and plum blossom waving outside our windows and the sight is glorious. The bullfinches, goldfinches, linnets and the memory of stepping out at night to listen to the nightingale and smell the blossom, draws my soul back like a magnet.

I've been busy wallpapering two of the bedrooms during the last month while Jim did the painting, but before I finish, I must tell you about the guest who replaced the lady we had to move on.

Mrs Wrackle arrived — small, neat, blue eyes, brown hair. She looked nearer 60 than 74 years of age. Very smart and active. All the guests seemed to like her except Mrs Ellen who was paralysed on one side, very independent and hated anyone fussing around her. We seat four guests to each round table and I had put Mrs Wrackle at Mrs Ellen's table. On the fourth day Rose told me that Mrs Ellen was cross and had said "Please, Mrs Wrackle do not interfere with me. Leave me alone. I'm quite capable of eating my meals without anyone fussing over me. It's embarrassing." Later, I praised Mrs Wrackle for her warm-heartedness, but begged her to leave Mrs Ellen alone, but she wouldn't, and I thought Mrs Ellen might have another stroke if this fussy woman continued to behave unreasonably. Then — you'll find this hard to believe — Rose reported that Mrs Wrackle was eating her soup with a fork! I went to the dining room and offered her a soup spoon. She refused it, and continued to slurp up the soup, which plopped back in the dish before she could get the fork in her mouth. Outside the dining room I said to Rose, "If this continues, I'll ask the doctor to examine her."

The next morning I was informed that she refused to get up and was very ill so I visited her, took her pulse and temperature, which were normal, and told her so.

"I'm seriously ill. I'll never get up again. I've got cancer of the liver — a bad heart — my kidneys have failed, so I shall never get out of bed again."

I tried to reason with her. First I said she'd dreamt it. Eventually I said, "The doctor gave you a clean bill of health before you arrived, so I must ask you to get up and get dressed and join the others. Come on Mrs Wrackle, they all like you. They'll miss your company."

The next minute I was struggling for my life. She leapt out of bed, grabbed me round the throat and banged the back of my head repeatedly on the door shouting, "I said I can't get out of bed. I'm dying. If anyone comes to this room I'll kill them like I'm going to kill you!"

I struggled free and once I'd got my senses back, phoned the doctor who got her removed within the hour. We were lucky a guest hadn't gone in to visit her. Take care of yourself. Looking forward to your next letter.

Much love,
Lillian.

24th JULY, 1965

Oh Tilly dear,

It was lovely to get your nice long letter and I did enjoy the phone calls we had and the advice you have given me. Phone calls are nice but at this distance apart they have to be brief, so I always think later, oh dear, I forgot to tell Tilly this, or forgot to tell Tilly that.

All of the guests seem happy at the moment. We've had lovely sunny days, with afternoon tea served on the lawn. Major Aldin and Colonel Sharp regale the ladies with stories. Some guests play bridge in the evening, others watch TV in the lounge and they have plenty of visitors. As I mentioned on the phone they can entertain guests from 7 am until midnight and, if any arrive during mealtimes and some guests have gone out to lunch, then I invite the visitors to join their relatives for a meal. This makes for happiness all round. We live like a big family and have made very good friends with some of the guests' relatives.

I must now relate the saga of Miss O'Hara. It all began with Derby week. Every morning she went down to the betting shop in the village and I was so busy that I didn't think it odd when I inspected the lunches, but on the Friday I went to inspect the cold larder to make sure it had been cleaned, and stared at a mass of rotting vegetables. The penny then dropped. We'd eaten tinned vegetables and fruit for five days, and the greengrocer was due with a fresh supply on the Saturday!

The next morning I braved Miss O'Hara, and pointed out the rotting vegetables and fruit.

"You've opened tinned vegetables and fruit every day and let this all go to waste. I trusted you so much Miss O'Hara," I said.

"Ah well, what's it all there for, if not to be used?" she said, pointing to the shelves of tinned fruit and vegetables. We argued for five minutes about the waste and eventually came to an agreement that she would look for another job, and that I would take over the cooking when she found one. I told her that I would be sorry to see her go, because as a cook she was excellent.

Well Tilly, I do wish you'd been in the kitchen on the following Sunday evening when Miss O'Hara arrived back at 10 pm. She'd been to evening Mass as usual and, as usual, called in at the local hostelry to enjoy her favourite tipple of Irish Whisky, or Paddy's eye-water as she called it. During the week she had asked me if I was going to marry Jim.

"Yes, but as he's not a Catholic like myself, it will be in a registry office," I replied.

17

She stood, swaying, with her hand on the door knob to keep her balance, and then made the following announcement:

"Haven't I been after thinking in church tonight? God sent me here for a purpose, and sure me eyes were opened while I prayed, for is it not to bring ye back in to the arms of the Church I was sent here? Now I'll tell ye what oi've decided, for don't I like this little job? It suits me very well, so you give up the Commander, come back to the Church and oi'll keep this little job, but I won't be after doing the breakfasts. It's a waste of good time boiling eggs, dishing up porridge and cereals, and making toast. Any fool can do that. It's not a cook's job at all. The staff can fry their own breakfasts for 'tis nothing to it. Come now. Say ye'll come back to the faith! What do you say to that?"

Tilly, I was almost speechless, but I just said, "You go to bed and have a good night's sleep, Miss O'Hara, and God bless you." When I repeated it to Jim five minutes later, I added that I would be sorry to see her go. She's a tremendous character, but oh the waste! Well, as I said, it was Derby week and she kept popping in to see the races on TV. One day she suddenly said, "Did you hear that now. He said Bar one! I always thought that horse would win." I found out that she'd had a little café in Dublin, and that they'd had to carry her out and put her in hospital for treatment, as she'd gone bankrupt. Her only problem had been her generosity.

I do look forward to your nice long newsy letters. I'm always telling Jim some anecdote about you and this week I recalled the dream I had about my wedding ring, high in the sky and seeming to encompass the earth, it broke in half. You remember how I worried every day and thought Roy might have an accident in the car, and of how he came home with the 'flu on the Friday and after an examination on the following Wednesday, I was told he'd got cancer of the thorax and couldn't live three weeks. I remember the specialist saying, "I'm sorry I can't wish you a happy Christmas." What a marvellous neighbour you turned out to be — a sister and a mother to me as well! The specialist's prediction turned out to be wrong. Between us we kept him happy, pain-free and unaware that he was going to die, for four months.

Remember? He'd said he was going to buy a wheelbarrow when he got better, and you sat with him after I'd shovelled all the horse manure left on the road on to the garden, and then left for Canterbury to buy a wheelbarrow, and do the Christmas shopping. I don't know who was most surprised — you and Roy at the sight of me trundling a red barrow full of parcels; myself at the marvellous display of plastic daffodils you'd unearthed from the eaves and set in the manure to surprise me; or your George, who'd spotted the manure whilst driving out, and hurried back to collect it, and saw what had happened to it.

18

Remember those last two weeks when Roy had to stay in bed, and you crept in each day and put a dinner ready for me to eat, in the oven! I owe you so much. I shall never be able to repay you, but the name Tilly fills me with a glow of love. May God help me to do for others as you have done for me.

Gosh! I haven't got up to anywhere near the 14 pages you often send me. Before I close I must tell you about the padre, as Jim calls him. He gives a service once a month in the lounge for the benefit of the people who can't go to church. The Roman Catholic priest does the same; they are both very kind, warm personalities, but the padre told us the funniest story I've heard for some time.

Jim and Mrs Hart (who, by the way, is registered as blind now) share the same birthday and all her relatives gathered for the great day — but she refused to let them pop the cork until Jim was present. It so happened that the padre was in the office and asked what was in the plastic bin.

"Home made whisky wine padre. Wait a minute, I'll get a bottle that's matured. It's very good."

I returned with the bottle and poured him half a glass. While drinking he asked for the recipe and had another glass, this time a full one. When he'd finished that he joined the party.

I served the lunch, keeping enough back to be served to Mrs Hart's family and ourselves an hour later, at which time the party broke up. As we escorted the padre though the hall, our parrot, Redvers, screeched a welcome at him, and our beaming padre said:

"What a fine parrot. He reminds me of the story of the two old ladies who kept two parrots and wanted to find out what sex they were. They took them to the vet who said, 'It's easy. When they mate, one bird will mount the other, so you put a piece of white ribbon around the neck of the bird that's on top and he will be the male'." A few weeks later the old ladies did this, and later invited the padre to tea. When he walked in the male parrot screeched, "I see they caught you at it too, padre!"

See what that home made whisky does for padres! And now, goodnight.

Much love,
Lillian.

19

30th NOVEMBER, 1965.

Dear Tilly,

I can imagine the delight you talked of in preparing for Christmas for Sweet Pea. That's what Christmas is about — children and loving. You ask what we're doing for Christmas. I will explain what preparations have been made.

Jim has ordered the tree, 14 feet tall, which will stand in the bay in the hall. Two nieces of the guests are going to help decorate it. We shall use holly and mistletoe to decorate the hall and lounges. Presents have been bought and wrapped. On two nights the guests will be entertained by carol singers and on another night by the Brownies, for whom we've also bought little presents. The Christmas cake and puddings are maturing. I'll ice the cake a few days before Christmas. We've arranged a Christmas party three days before Christmas as six of the guests will be going home to relatives, and we shall also have a New Year's party, as by that time the guests will have returned.

I pray that all our guests will keep well, as I've just spent a month getting up at 2 am, and again at 5 am, nursing a guest who'd been with us a long time. She died last week and a gentleman named Mr Howe has been booked in. I miss Miss Perrot who died. She was always so kind and gentle. She'd been a historian and a conversation with her was always interesting.

This Mr Howe seems quite deaf and refuses to sell his house as he said he prefers to live in his own house with a housekeeper. His daughters told me that not one had lasted a month until now, and they worried about him.

We were showing them around the guest's bedrooms which were unoccupied. It was 10.30 am and one guest had only recently got up, so it was the only bed not made.

One daughter said to me, "They do get their beds made don't they?"

"Of course," I replied, "this lady is a late riser, but her bed will soon be made up. As they all have a tray service breakfast in bed, they vary in the times they get up — but 10.30 am is the latest."

"Oh good, you like your bed made, don't you Dad?" said the daughter.

"Certainly not," he shouted, and with a red face he stamped off down the corridor. We all hurried after him and the second daughter asked him what was the matter. He said he was disgusted that they should say such a thing.

20

"What did I say?" asked the other daughter.

"You said I liked a bedmate." We calmed him down, but he still appeared tetchy. Men!

Actually they are quite nice. The ones we have here as guests (apart from the Colonel, Major and Padre) are a Scottish Mr McGregor, a German named Mr Shalk, and nice old Mr Croft who's been here six years.

Mr Croft is still paying what he paid four years ago. He's only got £1,000 behind him. A charitable society offered to pay his fees as they increased, if he would transfer his £1,000 to them. He stubbornly refused, however, saying he wanted to leave it to a nephew who has never visited him since he has been here!

Rose told me that she did all the washing and darning for a guest for four years — for nothing — before I came. He wore old clothes and told everyone he hadn't any money. He died and his nephew got £65,000! We see to the bed linen, but the guests send away their personal laundry, and he pleaded with Rose throughout the years that he couldn't afford to pay for laundry!

Miss McGregor frequently thanks us for looking after her father, but said it worries her to see so many ladies, as her father prefers men's company. We didn't tell her, but every night he sits and holds hands with a very attractive 68-year-old lady named Mrs Raidell, who suffers from arteriosclerosis. Mrs Raidell often comes down at 9 am and demands her breakfast which she has just had! I just say, "Come and have a cup of tea," and within two minutes she has forgotten what she came to the kitchen for.

The other afternoon we saw Mr McGregor with Mrs Raidell in his arms, and discreetly left them, but a couple of nights back she came to our lounge and asked where her daughter was.

"Valerie's in Somerset," I replied.

"Don't be stupid. I haven't got a daughter called Valerie. I wouldn't have given her a stupid name like that."

"Very well dear."

"Would you like a tot of sherry?" asked Jim. She beamed her acceptance, and I've got a funny feeling that Mrs Raidell will take more and more to enquiring where her daughter is in the evening.

We have a new member of staff. She came from the mental hospital as 'unemployable'. They tell me they have tried her in 40 jobs! Anne is golden-haired, blue-eyed, has a pretty Irish voice and is a very devout Catholic of about 40 years of age. She takes the trays in good time, but takes two hours to lay the dining room. Never mind, she's happy and fits in, but the other morning was a hoot. Jim brought a dead mole to the kitchen window and proceeded to describe the wonders of nature to the staff, when Anne's voice piped through the kitchen. "Ah, don't

21

we all know about the mole, for didn't Jesus say in the Bible, 'Cast the mole out of your eye'!"

This week I said, "Anne, you've been here three months. You have every afternoon and evening off, plus your day off, and you really must keep your bedroom tidier than you do."

"Ah sure, aren't you lucky to have an educated person like meself working for you," said Anne.

The other morning I asked her to wring the dish cloth harder, as all the trays were wet. She protested that her wrists were weak and she couldn't wring it any harder. Down in the cellar we keep surplus stores and some tinned foods and, later, I asked Anne to bring up five tins of peas. She came staggering into the kitchen with a carton of 24 tins, and was it heavy!

"Anne, you'll injure yourself. I just asked for five," I said.

"Ah sure, and what's the sense of running up and down the cellar every time you want a few tins?," she replied.

Look forward to all your news.

Much love,
Lillian.

15th DECEMBER, 1965

Tilly dear,

As you say, we are lucky to have a very efficient and faithful Rose, plus a hardworking loyal Jenny, because most of the local people earn big money in the factories in the towns, and don't want to know about domestic work. But I agree with you — I think I'd go crazy as well if I had to do the same job in a factory, day in day out. Jenny worked in a jam factory for 40 years after she left school at 14, and the only time she stayed home was for the birth of her baby daughter, which was looked after by her mother until Jenny and her husband came home from work. Jenny said she loved every minute in the factory, and hated it when she found herself living in this village without anything to occupy her time. Now she's happy again.

The new trainee cook arrived yesterday and she looked absolutely gormless — as if she'd find herself out if she called on herself. Fortunately, I made it strictly a week's trial. But perhaps she's not so gormless! I gave her oranges to squeeze for the breakfasts this morning and the glasses held only about half an inch of orange juice instead of one and a half to two inches. She'd eaten what was left on the skins! I will have to squeeze them myself tomorrow.

We dread another power cut, Tilly. The last time it meant being up all night, as the power station didn't manage to repair the damage until the next day. Everyone has a torch and we check the batteries regularly. We also have some electric lamps with big batteries, plus candles. We fix candles in every room and on all the landings, but we spend the night checking that nobody wanders round with a candle or walks off up the corridor with one — leaving it in darkness. One guest had removed two of the candles, leaving the corridor in darkness, and had three candles burning in her room!

Even when we've established that all guests are asleep, we can't relax in case anyone gets up. We hope to have emergency lighting installed one day, but the costs are so prohibitive that we must wait until we know we are sound enough financially to do it.

I found the trainee cook spooning all the parsley out of the sauce I'd shown her how to make.

"What are you doing?" I asked.

"It's got green flowers in," she said. I rang to tell the mental hospital that I was wasting my time, so they are taking her back today.

The Major told me yesterday that his first wife left him £200,000 and his second wife £100,000, but today he had his income tax demand, and said that they shouldn't charge him so much tax!

Mrs Hart hasn't been very well this week and I've had three weeks of getting up in the night to nurse dear Miss Dale who died, and the last three nights checking on Mrs Hart.

I said to Anne, "I'll pay you extra if you sit up for two hours with Mrs Hart so I can get a rest in the afternoon." Mrs Hart's daughter came in and found Mrs Hart in the chair and Anne asleep on her bed!

Fiona came to Jim and said, "Really, Jim darling, Anne was asleep on Mummy's bed." I took Anne to apologise to Fiona and to tell her it wouldn't happen again.

"Ah sure, 'tis sorry I am, but didn't your mother herself tell me to lie on the bed when I said I was tired," said Anne. Thank goodness Mrs Hart shows signs of getting better now. She assured her daughter that she had insisted on Anne lying down.

Oh, I could weep Tilly. The gardener saw dear Nyger fall off the roof. We carried him in in a blanket and called for the vet who put him to sleep. Dear, dear Nyger. He was an affectionate cat and loved by all the guests. We didn't tell the guests or staff so that nobody would get as upset as us.

Animals, Tilly, you can trust them; they never let you down. They don't worry about whether you're rich or poor, good-looking or plain. They're loyal.

We were amused last week when the owner of the general stores and off-licence in the village said to Jenny, "When you're going to work tomorrow, deliver this bottle of whisky to Mr Fine." Jenny delivered it to Mr Fine.

The next day Mr Ray, the owner of the shop, said to Jenny, "Did you deliver the bottle of whisky to Mr McGregor?"

"No, I gave it to Mr Fine. That's who you told me to give it to. I'll get it back and give it to Mr McGregor this morning." When she went to his room she found he'd drunk two thirds of it!

"You'd better give me the money to buy another bottle for Mr McGregor," said Jenny, after she'd explained her mistake.

"Certainly not! If he ordered it, let him pay for it," said Mr Fine, who suffered from frequent lapses of memory.

Jenny reported back to Mr Ray who came up to explain to Mr Fine how the mistake had occurred. (Mr Fine used to order a crate of beer and a bottle of rum once a week). Climbing the stairs I met an angry Mr Ray who was shouting over his shoulder, "That's the last delivery you get from me." I invited him into the office and explained how difficult Mr Fine could be. I told him not to take any notice, and that we would get the money back. He calmed down after we'd explained what we'd gone through where money was concerned. We paid him and said we'd get the money back, and he promised to continue to deliver the drinks to him.

Last year, Tilly, when Jim presented Mr Fine with the bill for April to May, which ran from April 18, instead of paying on the dot (as he always did) he left it, and within a few days Jim called him to the office to remind him that he hadn't paid.

"Oh, but I have Guv'nor. Here's the proof. Look. Paid to April 18, I paid you on April 18."

Jim said, "You did, but the new bill is due for May."

We argued and argued but didn't get anywhere, so we phoned his bank manager who said, "Don't worry. It's his birthday next week. I'll call in and get him to sign a standing order, and the problem will disappear."

The next week the bank manager spent an hour with him, explaining that he wanted to help him make life easy. As soon as he said "Sign here and you won't have the worry of signing cheques", Mr Fine stood up and said, "Do you mind? You're interfering with my dinner," and marched off.

Afterwards the manager said to me, "Well, you'll get it sometime, but it's up to you now to think of something." Three months passed and he refused to pay each bill, irrespective of the dates. He always kept the bills, paid or otherwise, on his dressing table underneath a small box. They all looked tatty, with the corners turned down. I thought, "supposing I remove the last three unpaid bills and present him with an undated bill?" We did. It worked. He presented us with a cheque for the month.

We rang the bank manager who agreed that we'd better do the same to get the other two unpaid bills. We did, and he paid the three bills in a week without a murmur. We presented him with a bill for the price of the whisky, and remembered not to mention whisky, and he paid this as well.

There were another couple of incidents that I didn't bother to tell Mr Ray about. Mr Fine asked Rose to collect his pension, and it turned out he hadn't collected it for six months. They told Rose that he couldn't claim back six months' pension unless there was a special reason, and only a relative could then claim it in that case. Rose felt sorry for him and, claiming she was a relative, made five costly journeys to the Department of National Insurance, filled in forms, and eventually gave him six months back pension.

"I must reward you," he said and unlocking his wardrobe gave her a peppermint! If he hadn't given her the peppermint which caused her to collapse with laughter, we wouldn't have known about it.

The next week Rose said to him, "We don't want to go through all that trouble in claiming your pension Mr Fine, so give me your book, and I'll collect it tomorrow."

"Certainly not! Be off with you," said Mr Fine.

Jenny went in (within seconds) with a pair of socks she'd darned for him.

"Have you got a lipstick you can lend me?" he asked Jenny.

"Yes, I'll get you one," she said, puzzled.

When Rose returned with the waste paper basket she saw, written in lipstick all over the mirror, "We'll have no petticoat government around here." He was the only one never to have given Rose a Christmas present, but when Rose was in hospital having an operation, the builders who were working outside his room warned me that he was giving the 23-year-old girl (who was doing a temporary job while Rose was away) £5 per day. Immediately I gave the relief Jenny's rooms to clear, and gave Jenny Rose's rooms to clear, without giving Jenny any details of what I'd heard, but explaining that she'd have her rooms back when Rose was back.

He was quite a character, and liked by all, and the niece who arranged for him to come here is a treasure. The first week he arrived he gave notice, and said the people were too old. He was 90 years of age. Then within another week he said, "I'll never leave here, it's home from home." He's now 94 and said to the niece last week, "You only visit me because you're after my money." He's forgotten that she is a trustee to see that it all goes to The Salvation Army, where it will do a lot of good.

Ah, Tilly, wouldn't life be dull if we were all the same, my love.

May peace and joy be with you all this Christmas. Thank you for the gold pixies.

Much love,
Lillian.

23rd JANUARY, 1966

Oh Tilly,

What a Christmas! It was all go, but everyone enjoyed themselves. The high spots were as follows.

Number one, the Brownies! After they finished singing carols they all sat on the floor and sang and mimed camp songs. The Christmas party was a great success. Mr Croft refused to come down, saying he was too old, but he was eventually persuaded to change his mind. One drink later he got up and danced and sang Any old Iron! We had a pianist, Jim sang and got them all singing. He has a fine voice and they kept asking for an encore.

Friends came and helped and we got everyone tucked up in bed by 10.30 and then we continued to celebrate until 1 am.

This was duplicated on New Year's Eve with gusto. First I prepared a hot punch of vodka, white wine and peach juice. Jim entered dressed only in a white sheet, carrying a scythe in one hand and an hour glass (actually a giant egg-timer) in the other. Rose announced Father Time and proclaimed that the New Year was coming in. Then they pushed me in in a pram. I had a frilly bathmat on my head, and there was a balloon blown up through a ring of cardboard, which represented the dummy. There was singing and dancing until 10 o'clock when Jim whispered that some looked sleepy, and we'd all better make a move to help the guests to bed. It was in that moment's silence that the unexpected happened.

We'd made friends with two neighbours who were millionaires. As we couldn't go out in the evenings, they often came over for an hour. He's 60 and she's 70 years of age. When sober she's the biggest prude you can imagine, but when high on champagne, which she often is by 10 o'clock in the morning, she's outrageously embarrassing. She was sitting between 91-year-old Mrs Hart and 95-year-old Mr Shalk when she suddenly said, "I like sex!"

"What did you say, you've got six?" asked Mrs Hart.

"No. I said I like sex," she said loudly and adamantly. Suddenly everyone spoke at once and we all hastened to escort the guests to their rooms. We laughed at it later. But while I'm writing about them, I must tell you what happened six weeks ago. I wished the floor had opened at the time. It was so embarrassing.

We had friends from London to dinner in the evening, and I've noticed before that Jack always rings up and makes the excuse that Yvonne's ill and would I come and look at her. Then he comes over to join our company for an hour. If that happens when there's a couple with us, I usually take the wife along with me. This night we sat in their lounge, which is like a 30 foot by 50 foot goldfish bowl, with windows on three sides, big logs burning in the fireplace, and chaise-longues about 15 feet apart. I felt I needed a microphone to make our friend Alison hear, as she was sitting on a chaise-longue on the far side of the room. Yvonne was stretched out on another, the other side of the fireplace.

We exchanged a few pleasantries and then the perfect silence was disturbed as Yvonne said, "My sex life is perfect now and it's all due to you. All the hints and tips and advice you gave me. We made love from six o'clock until 10 o'clock this morning."

I couldn't speak! She'd obviously been on the bottle all day. I went to the phone and asked Jack to come back and after he arrived I bid them goodnight, and we walked back. I didn't say anything. I felt so annoyed.

Two weeks later Alison and John came to dinner again and mentioned Yvonne.

"Oh, don't remind me about her. I've never discussed sex with her," I said.

Alison said, "We know, we laughed all the way back to London. Your face was a picture. It made an unforgettable night for us."

Now for the sad news. We had a new guest last year, a Mrs Flint. She made friends with Mr Croft and Mrs Hargreaves, an ex-nurse who had had a stroke and who had been here six years. Mrs Flint put a letter in the office to us on New Year's Day, informing us that she didn't think it fair that Mr Croft was paying £8 a week and that she was paying £20 a week. If we didn't reduce her to £8 a week she would leave. She received a carefully drafted letter explaining that each guest's circumstances were different (and private) and also that the price varied with the type of room, and she had one of the best in the establishment. We said we would regret it if she left, and hoped she would reconsider.

She asked Mrs Hargreaves to accompany her to see the matron of a nursing home the next day, and when they returned they *both* gave notice! Mrs Hargreaves has always complained that she was short of money and has currently been paying £14 per week. We said we would be sorry to lose her and would miss her. It was her sixth year here.

At the end of the week she left with Mrs Flint, and a week later we got a tearful letter asking us for her room back. She said she hadn't realised that she would have to pay £35 per week and share with three other people; the gas fire was put on for them to dress and again to undress, but not kept on all day. Anyway, she was stuck in the same room, as it was a nursing home.

I phoned the matron and arranged for her return.

The matron said, "I've got rid of that other one, Mrs Flint. She did nothing but complain, and I can fill this place any time I want to."

The day she was to come back, Mrs Hargreaves fell from the top to the bottom of the stairs — and that was the end for her.

Three days later, on Anne's day off, I took the breakfasts round, and was greeted happily by a smiling Mr Croft. When I returned to collect the tray, I could hear a strange sound coming from the room before I got there. He had had a massive cerebral haemorrhage and I phoned the doctor, who came at once. Mr Croft died while we were waiting for the ambulance. It's an awfully sad story, Tilly, and it caused us to discuss what happens to other people that we can never know about. There must be millions of sad or humorous stories to be told by people who have run homes, whether private or local authority.

More news. I interviewed an Irish cook of 30 years of age who has been working in a nursing home. She starts next week. The day before *we* had been interviewed by a cook! We paid her expenses to come up from the south coast. She arrived — all six foot of her — dressed in tweeds. I excused myself as one of the guests was in trouble. The prunes had upset his tummy and, as he is paralysed on one side, he needed help changing. Fifteen minutes later I apologised for keeping her waiting, and asked her if she would like a cup of tea.

"I am not accustomed to being kept waiting. Do you want to interview me, or don't you?" she thundered. I apologised again, and poured boiling water on to the tea. which she eventually accepted.

"Cigarette?" I asked.

"Roll me own," she snapped, and produced a tin box and proceeded to roll her own! "How many staff will I have to help?" she asked.

"One," I replied.

"Nonsense, I'll have to have more than that. How many guests have you got?"

We continued answering her questions and I grew more sorry for her as each minute passed. She must have been a good 70 years of age. We paid her, gave her something extra for her trouble, and sighed with relief when she had gone. It's silly, but I could have cried. She looked as though she needed looking after.

The Spring will soon arrive. Already one notices the light a little earlier in the mornings, and you will soon enjoy all your lovely blossom. Take care of yourself.

Much love,
Lillian.

P.S. Mr Croft's body was in the mortuary for six days while they tried unsuccessfully to contact the nephew.

10th MAY, 1966.

Surprise! Surprise! Tilly my Love,

Yesterday we got married! We didn't tell anyone except Peggy and Mrs Hart's daughter, as we did not want people to spend money on dressing up, or on buying presents that they could not afford. It caused great excitement here. Two days before the great day arrived, the wedding cake arrived unexpectedly while we were shopping. We returned to find a very red-faced angry Yorkshire Jenny. She strode into the office and let forth.

"Here, Commander. I've worked for you all these years, and I don't know how you could do this to me?"

Jim asked, "Do what?"

"Go and get married and not tell me. Ee ba gum, I feel so hurt."

"Listen Jenny, nobody's to know. You're the first, and if you tell anyone, we're finished, you and I."

We calmed her down and proceeded to make arrangements for the reception.

Canapes in the lounge with champagne at 11.30 am. All guests to be sitting in the lounge ready for us to hand round the champagne. Nothing turns out exactly as one plans. Rose stood at the head of the stairs and cried with Jim's aunt. She said Jim looked so happy.

Peggy and Nobby arrived and we all went to the registry office. We returned to be greeted by all the staff in the porch with the finest wedding bouquet we have ever seen — masses of deep red and white carnations. It so happened that Rose remembered that one of the guest's sons owned a florist's shop. She rang and ordered it after we had left. They opened the door to the hall and there stood all the guests to give three rousing cheers!

In the lounge the corks popped and we were just about to cut the cake when our doctor arrived.

"There isn't anyone ill," I said, puzzled.

"Ah, a little dicky bird told me about today, and I wanted to wish you all the happiness that my wife and I have had," he said. I felt overwhelmed.

At one o'clock the guests went in to lunch, and we sat down with Peggy and Nobby and Mrs Hart's daughter at a table that was specially laid in the lounge. Our old lady doctor, Dobbs, joined us at the table and insisted that her dinner was served with ours. We agreed. By the way, this Dr Dobbs has forgotten nearly everything she ever learned, but she still has prescription pads, and makes out prescriptions for the guests behind our backs! We have had a word with the chemist, who makes sure they are not made up.

The other day we had a disaster. The landing had been newly carpeted throughout with a beautiful blue carpet. Miss Jane used the red bathroom and left a trail of faeces along the whole length of it. She cried. I washed her and reassured her that accidents happen to us all, while dear Rose heaved away with rubber gloves until she got it back to its original immaculate state. I asked her what she had taken. It turned out that five guests had given her different aperients within 48 hours, and — to crown it all — Dr Dobbs gave her 10 Senokot, and told her that they did not work unless you take the lot at once! From now on I will see that everyone has to come to the office for aperients.

Well, Tilly, back to the wedding. We celebrated all day and we were joined by John and Alison, and by Jack and Yvonne later. It ended with Jim falling asleep, sitting up on the settee. I had to wake him, and we checked everything was safe before going to bed. The only thing missing that day was you.

Now the cook. The first day she started at 12.30 pm. I checked the kitchen and there were 28 bloody, half-cooked chops in the bottom of the Rayburn.

"You've not cooked chops before Cook. Look at them!"

As I pointed to them, she agreed.

"Oh dear!" I said.

I would like to teach her, and I must say she is learning quickly, but she told me that the owner of the previous nursing home used to buy bags of outside cabbage leaves to be cooked for the patients, and, in any case, it was mostly fish or mince that was cooked! We learn something new every day, don't we?

Talking of cooking reminds me. My sister-in-law used to do a marvellous jugged hare. I have never cooked one, but the other day I saw a row of hares in a butcher's shop and, remembering the delicious flavour, I bought five. First I had to skin them. Having skinned rabbits, I thought it would be easy, but I think some cunning sprite had put "Uhu glue" in the wombs as I wrestled with them for over an hour. Then came the disjointing! Knife, hammer and saw did not seem to have much effect, so I got an axe. Another hour and a half later the cook, followed by Anne and Mary, arrived in the kitchen. Their faces registered disbelief as they saw all the blood on the floor, the table, the walls and myself!

The next day I removed from the oven a dark gooey mess.

"I don't want any," said Jim.

"Nor me," "Nor me," "Nor me," "Nor me," said the staff.

"Nor me either," I thought. "But I can't waste it, look what they cost — and a bottle of Nuits St George to marinate them in!"

31

"What? You never used a bottle of Nuits St George. You're mad!" Jim exploded.

I said, "I'll apologise to them when you serve the pudding Anne." I went in with her and, would you believe it, the plates were clean except for bones — and they all praised it! I'll never buy hares again, but here is a story in reverse.

I told the cook I would show her how I made risotto, and that we would have it for the evening meal. Rice, four pounds of mince, tomatoes, tomato puree, Oxos, butter and mushrooms produced a very tasty risotto, which cooked in a slow oven throughout the afternoon. Cook tasted it and said she would sit and eat her share there and then, it was so good. The other staff said the same, and so did Jim.

At seven o'clock Anne brought the empty soup plates back, and served the risotto. Every plate came back untouched. Anne said that Mrs Brownlow, the padre's widow, said, "Take it away, I'm not eating that foreign muck," and put everyone else off. The next time I produce a new dish, I'll talk to them first and whet their appetites. Greek Dolmathers are out of this world, but I would hate to waste the hours it takes to make them to perfection, and see them go to waste.

The padre came in yesterday and told us he is having trouble with his 94-year-old father who keeps getting up at two o'clock in the morning and begins to fry his breakfast, insisting it is 8 am. He also uses the padre's shoes to urinate in if the padre forgets to put them away. He asked the doctor for stronger sleeping pills for his father, but they haven't had much effect. He said he was so tired the other night he decided to take some himself and try to get a good night's sleep!

We have a new guest — a very attractive 60-year-old, Mrs Davies. She is very with it in the way of fashion and make-up. She has been in a mental hospital since the death of her husband and within the last three years has had both breasts removed, and the womb. Each morning she has a bout of tears, and I reassure her that everyone loves her and she will be happy. She spends most of the morning applying mascara and lipstick. The other day, after returning from shopping with two new dresses, she cut the hems off and now they are four inches above the knee!

The son asked me to watch her carefully, as she once ran off from the hospital with a 19-year-old boy, and he had to fetch her back. She has told all the women that she had to go to hospital as a result of a breakdown after having the breasts removed.

Normally, all is reasonably peaceful here, but the other morning I heard the Colonel's voice booming down in the hall.

"Woman, keep your dirty mouth shut, and don't speak to me again."

I rushed down to enquire what the trouble was. He was reluctant to

32

tell me, but finally did. He often gives a little cocktail party to several of the guests, including Mrs Davies. The padre's widow, Mrs Brownlow, had gone to his room and said, "I think I ought to warn you that you shouldn't entertain Mrs Davies in your room. She is diseased."

Good for the Colonel! What say you?

We had to smile when Mrs Hart returned from hospital and heard from the other guests that Mrs Brownlow had been sitting with Mr Shalk every afternoon. She stamped her foot in rage.

"If he wants the company of a woman like that he doesn't get entertained by me any more," she said. The daughter and Jim managed to persuade her that she was tops in Mr Shalk's eyes, and all is well. He is back on the cocktail list. Mind you, he is sharp. Mrs Brownlow is the most gifted needlewoman, and is always ready to do any repairs for the men!

I have gone on long enough now, Tilly, and I'm looking forward to all your news. Love to all. I've decided to sell the house, so I will phone you with the details.

Much love,
Lillian.

Tilly dear,

I'm glad you like your new neighbour and hope it is the beginning of a long friendship for you all. You have had lots of happy things happen this year, and I'm sure you've got plenty more to come.

We have had an argument. I was telling Jim that occasionally I had dreams that come true.

He said, "Nonsense. People read things into dreams after the event has taken place."

Very well, I'll write down my dreams every morning in the business diary and then we will be able to check back, because each page will later be filled with the events of the day.

I quoted many dreams that I have had that came true, but you know Tilly, William Blake wrote, "He who doubts from what he sees will ne're believe, do what you please". He will believe one day, though. We all dream five or six times a night whether we recall the dreams or not.

We had a shock over Joan, as I told you briefly over the phone. Here is a more detailed account. When Miss O'Hara was cook, the milk seemed to go down rapidly every few days. But when she left, and until Maureen the new cook started, there was ample in the fridge. We take 16 pints a day, and 32 on Saturday. I warned the cook to keep an eye on the milk as it was a mystery to me how it had disappeared in her predecessor's time.

The first Saturday the cook was here she asked Jenny to check the 32 pints in the kitchen before she went off duty. I watched them through the open hatch in the office. Five minutes later Joan came into the kitchen and walked into the staff room. I heard and observed her make several trips into the kitchen and out through the back door. At 3.40 pm the cook came back with Anne and came straight into the office. She asked me to check the milk. There were 12 pints missing! Jim and I discussed this later. There wasn't any doubt that it was Joan. But why?

We'd taken on another help from the hospital a month before. She was named Jean. There had also been a lot of breakages for which we couldn't find the cause. You remember the beautiful Meissen birds Roy gave me? I put them in the guests' lounge to give them pleasure, but found them smashed to smithereens, and I had not got them insured. Jim said to stop worrying and sleep on it, then have a word with the social worker about it. I'd got up at five am to make sure Mrs

Jeeves did not need changing and it was such a lovely morning I strolled around the garden after attending to her. As I approached the windows of our lounge I saw Joan inside, with her back to me. She took an ornate china antique bowl off a shelf and, placing it on the floor, she ground it to pieces with her heel.

I phoned the social worker and hospital, and explained the situation. The social worker came over straight away. Over coffee with Jim and I, she told us that Joan left her husband and got a job in a general hospital. Six months later they noticed there were a lot of serious breakages. They set a trap and caught Joan at it. She did this whenever the matron praised anyone. So they had her admitted to a mental hospital!

"Why didn't you tell me this when you first brought her?" asked Jim.

"We're not allowed to, in case it would prejudice her chances," she replied. Joan was duly removed, and we took on two more staff from the hospital, Mai and Thelma.

Mai walked out at the end of the first week saying, "I'm going home to my brother. This place is too big for me."

A few days later I had a phone call from the hospital informing me that a tearful Mai was back in, asking to be sent back here because she liked us. She's back!

Thelma was an attractive 30-year-old mother of three children but found the strain of rearing them too much, and had had a breakdown. Now that she was better she wanted to work, preferably to train as a cook. Her first day was cook's day off and I showed her how to make custard and left her stirring it. When I returned to the kitchen she was staring out of the window. The kitchen was black with smoke, and the saucepan burnt through!

The next day I asked her if she could clean windows.

"Yes," she said.

"Don't attempt to open those curved ones in the ballroom. They have been here 300 years and we might not get them shut again," I told her.

Twenty minutes later a white-faced Jim yelled, "Get that blasted girl away from the windows. She's opened one." It took Jim and the gardener an hour to get it back.

The following day I gave her carpet-sweeping to do and, as Anne was having her day off, Jim served the lunch. As he was about to lift the tray, Thelma pushed a magazine showing the picture of a nude woman under his nose.

"Don't you think that is very artistic?" she asked Jim.

"Give that to me," I said, and rushed to her room to leave it on her dressing table. There I saw an open letter with an envelope beside it

35

addressed to the Pope. She told him that her husband was a homosexual; that she had fallen in love with the parish priest, and would he
give a dispensation for them to be married. She said she desperately
wanted to get out of this place because the Spanish nuns tied her down
to the bed every night! You've guessed right, Tilly. I phoned the social
worker and got her removed at once! The difficulty today is getting
anyone that is capable and efficient to live on a job where elderly
people need attention. I had to take on as relief, a young married
woman with a four-year-old child while the staff had holidays. She had
lived in a furnished house in the village during the previous 12
months, having come from Glasgow because her husband had got a
job in the car industry. I made sure she knew it was only for two
months, and agreed to let her bring the child.

The first week all was well, but on the Monday of the second week I
said, "Right Kate, I'll go on ahead and put all the clean linen on each
landing if you will start on the North Wing."

Beginning on the North Wing I stacked clean towels and sheets on
the window sills opposite each door and continued on to the main
building. Coming back through the swing door 20 minutes later, I saw
the linen untouched. I found Kate and her child sitting in the kitchen
half way through bacon and eggs.

"What's this?" I asked.

"They're entitled to have a breakfast if they work here. You can't
expect them to work on an empty stomach," said the cook.

"What?" I exploded. I reminded her exactly what the terms of
employment were and said she could leave then if she wished, but
there wasn't a shop, factory, office or local authority home where she
could be hired for three hours work and begin by eating a cooked
breakfast. Ten minutes later she came to me, apologised, and said I
was right. She worked the eight weeks and I said I hoped she would get
another job that suited her, and that if she was free during the next
holiday season I would be pleased to offer her the job again.

At five o'clock that afternoon a dark-haired slim man in his 30s
appeared on the doorstep and demanded two months' wages for his
wife in lieu of notice. We argued for five minutes and then I told him I
would call the police if he didn't leave. The following Monday the local
publican came to see me because he had rented one of his houses to
them, and they had cleared off to Scotland on the Friday night owing
him two months unpaid rent. Rose came to me at noon the same day
and asked me what had happened to three of the new cellular white
blankets. After an investigation it appeared that Kate had asked Jenny
and cook if it was all right to take the spare newspapers for her fire, and
was seen to make off with a large basketful of what appeared to be
newspapers each day.

Well, the girl had some good in her. I received a letter out of the blue this week apologising for her behaviour and telling me that I had been a kind employer.

There is not much time left to write about the guests. I'll tell you more in the next letter. I'll also phone as promised.

Much love,
Lillian.

15th JULY, 1966

Tilly dear,

Sorry I had to break off on that last phone call, I heard a bell ring. It was Mrs Hart. She said she heard a bang above her head. I investigated and found Mr Toller had had a heart attack. He has recovered now, but he badly burnt his hand on the radiator. He must have grabbed it as he hit the floor. I wouldn't have thought anyone could have burnt themselves so badly from an oil-fired central heating radiator, but the skin is fragile on an elderly person.

I'm writing this in the office, during which time five guests have come in with shopping lists. Each one said, "There's no hurry," but I must laugh, because for three of those five, "There's no hurry" means now or sooner, as they will repeatedly come back to see if their shopping has arrived. Patience and a sense of humour is all that's needed — and Jim needed it this week.

The Colonel threw what appeared to be 500 razor blades out of his window on to the lawn, and then stubbed cigarettes out in several pot plants in the hall. The padre stuffed rotten oranges down the toilet and we had to have the plumbers in. Then came the episode over Caeser the cat. Dear Caeser sat on the red formica top at the far end of the kitchen where the other three cats get fed. I passed in and out during the morning wondering where he had been, thinking he looked wet. His magnificent Persian coat glistened as if he had been in the bath. At 4 pm the sun was shining, and I heard Jim call out, "Quickly, come quickly, we must phone the vet!" I rushed out on to the lawn and couldn't believe my eyes. Caeser's coat had set into hard black enamel.

"I painted the gutters that run through the attics with black aquaseal yesterday. I do it every second year. He has been through them. Phone the vet while I catch him," said Jim.

The vet said, "He must be brought in, or it will kill him," so I went back to the kitchen with the cat basket, but there was no sign of Caeser or Jim. I don't know if he was psychic, but he led us a dance. It was nearly half past five when we caught him and put him in the cat basket.

"Just a minute Jim," I said, "his tail's sticking out," As I slightly raised the lid, Caeser was quicker than either of us. He sprang out and disappeared through the cat-flap. Jim swore, and off we went in pursuit of Caeser! At 6 pm the cook called through the window, "The vet is on the phone." I rushed in and explained the situation. He said he couldn't go home until I had brought him in, and would we please hurry up.

"Put some meat on a piece of string." "Open a tin of salmon." Suggestions poured in thick and fast from both guests and staff, who were all in on the trap Caeser act.

"Let's all go in and ignore him, and you sit on a chair by the side of the cat-flap to prevent him escaping again if he comes in," I said. Fifteen minutes later we heard a cry "He's in" and within five minutes we were driving off to the vet, me silent, Rose wasn't and Jim red-faced and furious!

The vet worked furiously, pouring a liquid on the coat and rubbing him with a white towel that soon turned black. About 20 black towels later he began to clip off Caeser's coat, and we returned with a very forlorn and mangy looking Caeser.

". . . but there was no sign of Caeser."

Rose was amused when I told her that snooty Mrs Smythe Robinson came to the lounge door twice the other night and demanded that Miss Osborne be made to sit in the lounge instead of the hall.

"She's sitting on the other side of Mr McGregor and trying to take him away from Mrs Raidell," she said.

Jim spoke sharply, "Nonsense, Mrs Smythe Robinson. The hall is free to all guests. This is the second time you've made this silly complaint and I don't want to hear about it again."

I said he shouldn't have spoken so abruptly as she suffers from heart attacks. It worried me when I went into the hall and found she had gone to bed, so I went to her bedroom where I found her sitting on the bed with a glass of sherry in one hand and a cigarette in the other.

"You've come to bed early. Are you all right?" I asked. "Oh, Lamb, of course I'm all right. What a wonderful man your husband is. He reminds me of my Jack. What a lot he has to put up with, with all us foolish old women."

The next day she came into the office, and informed me that she was going to give notice if I didn't get rid of Miss Osborne!

"I will regret that," I replied. "I do not intend to give Miss Osborne notice, so if you insist on giving yours, that will be our loss, Mrs Smythe Robinson."

She stared at me for a few minutes and then walked out and closed the door. Ten minutes later she was back.

"I've been a bit silly, Lamb. I won't be leaving," she announced.

"Tell me, Mrs Smythe Robinson, why don't you like Miss Osborne? She's quiet, polite, and never interferes with you."

"She's not a lady."

"What is your definition of a lady?" I asked.

"A person who is educated," was the astonishing reply.

"Then Miss Osborne is truly acceptable. She was an Oxford graduate. You weren't, and you're judging her by her appearance — casual loose shirts, and a bun at the back of her head!"

She seemed to go white.

"Come now, Mrs Smythe Robinson, we all love you. You go and talk to Miss Osborne, you'll probably end up loving her." I kissed her and all seems peaceful now.

Rose said, "Perhaps you will have another wedding if Mr McGregor proposes to Mrs Raidall. We've had one big wedding here, when Dr Rhys Davies married Miss Lord."

"No, Rose! When?"

"About four years ago. He was 91 and she was a spinster of 65. The next morning I took their breakfasts up. He was sitting up as usual with an old-fashioned nightcap on his head, and she sat up beside him with a pretty pink frilly bedjacket over a white satin nightgown. She looked glowing. When I told them in the kitchen they all begged me to let them collect the trays but I wouldn't have them embarrassed."

"Well, I'm blessed. Jim never told me about that," I explained. "So much has happened since. Anyway, he bought her a house and they moved within three months. He died six months later. She still visits Mrs Green in the flat. Haven't you met her?"

"No."

"You will, she's all right".

Well, Tilly, I wouldn't be surprised at anything after that.

I nearly forgot! While I've got time, I must tell you about the electric meter episode. Nearly 12 months ago we had a letter from the electricity board telling us that we must pay eight pence per unit from 8 am until 8 pm as we were a business. Up until that time all the large bedrooms measuring 30 square feet or more, had electric fires in them, as even with the central heating full on we couldn't get them above 60 degrees, whereas the smaller rooms reached 78 degrees. If the guests felt chilly they just had to switch on freely. Jim called in a man from the board for advice, as he said people are absent minded and often leave them on in the summer.

"Put meters in those six rooms," he advised.

It was arranged that we paid four pence out of each shilling put in, and so an army of machines was installed to register the switch over, and six meters installed. In one large room on the ground floor, a guest named Mrs James burnt the fire throughout the day, even in the summer this year. Rose complained the room was overheated, but of the other five rooms, four refused to put the heaters on, complaining that it cost money! Mrs James's daughter, a lawyer's wife, visited her every morning and stayed about ten minutes. I thought it was so nice to see a daughter keep a careful and loving eye on her mother. Every couple of months I'd take the key, open the meters, and collect what money I found inside. After the first three months I found money in only one meter, and that was nearly full. Mrs James's meter had only ten shillings in it and each time I thought "Jim has emptied this one". With so much to do I never mentioned this to him, but just locked the money in the cash drawer for him to sort out.

Three weeks ago Mrs James's daughter went away for a holiday. On the second evening, Mrs James asked me to empty the meter and refill it!

"No, Mrs James, you give me a £1 note and I'll give you 20 shillings."

She remained adamant that the money was taken out and replaced, and we had the same conversation every other night, until the end of the week, when I mentioned it to Jim. He said he had never emptied the meter. We inspected it, and found the screws were missing. You could lift it off and, by pushing the shilling in and clicking the base, it dropped and registered. So we decided to have the meter sealed.

The first day after the daughter arrived back from holiday she called in to see her mother as Rose was making the mother's bed. When she had finished Mrs James said, "I've had to put a lot of money in that meter. They won't let me take it out and put it in again."

The daughter rushed over to the meter, spotted it was sealed and, straightening up, said sharply to her mother, "The Commander said you can't have the heating on in this room again."

Rose reported this immediately. I called Jim, and we asked her to see us in the office before leaving. She nodded her head in dismay when we told her that if it was very cold, and the mother decided to sit in her room instead of the hall or lounge, we would put money in the meter and keep an account of it, and give it to her once a month to settle. You should have seen her face, knowing we had bowled her out! It worked out that we had been subsidising the mother for 12 months. What a dirty trick!

When I was a hotel manageress I had some shocks about the dishonesty of both guests and staff, but although it is a bigger shock to find it among the aged or their relations, I think what a joy it is to know that there are millions of very honest and loving people in the world, like many of our guests and staff. We also think of what problems other people face in the running of homes, both private and local authority. Here we don't have first, second or third class stomachs. We all eat the same, and we live as one big family; each with the right to privacy when it is needed, and with mutual respect and courtesy.

What a joy it is to get back from a rare day's shopping in London! After a quick cup of tea, everyone wants to know what I did. Mrs Hart tells me that she worries when I'm out in case of an accident, and the place seems quiet without me. They make me feel like a loved daughter. Whatever will the world be like when we are old, Tilly? Every one is being told that we are all equal and we all have rights. They don't talk about responsibilities and love. Thank God we're all unequal! What a dull world it would be if we were all carbon copies. Every time I hear or read about an Ecclesiastic preaching about equality, or pushing his nose into politics, I puke. Jesus washed the feet of the disciples; that great act of love and humility which has ennobled the lives of millions down through the centuries. Today the clergy talk like Marx. They talk instead of doing.

I do seem to have gone on and on. I shall be looking forward to hearing that you have won the battle to keep cars from parking either end of the unmade road, so that you can drive out freely again.

Much love,
Lillian.

42

Tilly dear,

What a joy to know that at last you've won the battle to keep the cars from parking. I agree it must have been annoying to find you were stuck for hours until the farmer's wife or children drove off again. You have asked me to come and stay with you for holidays, and there is nothing I'd like better, but I don't see us getting one this year. There is still a lot of decorating to be done — but you must come here when you can.

It has been a busy time. We have had our usual inspection. The health office pronounced everything perfect! The fire officers and their men carried out their annual visit, but this time it was funny. They have to make sure they know where the water hydrants are, and once they've fixed the hoses they always have a trial display.

It was 7.30 in the evening and Mrs Blous was standing with the window wide open taking fresh air, when she got drenched from head to foot. I ran up and changed her. The firemen apologised, and she had a good laugh and came down to enjoy a tot of whisky with them all.

The next week the nursing officer made her inspection and it was her first visit here. The last one was exceptionally nice, and this one wasn't unpleasant, but she annoyed me. I took her to every room where she said, "Good morning, keeping well, are we? What are you doing?"

After we had visited 21 rooms, we went to the kitchen and the phone rang. I answered it and when I returned I overheard her talking to the cook.

"Now you must be sure to give them plenty of fresh fruit every day. It's very important!"

Tilly, I ask you! She'd seen fresh fruit in almost every room, the stupid so and so. Incidentally, the chief officer of the local health department has his father here, so they know what the standard is.

Probably what I found irritating, was the implication that they were either children or gaga. I mean, "Keeping well are we?"! Last year the nursing officer took a different approach.

She said, "You are Mrs --------. I'm so pleased to meet you," or "I've come round again to find out what sort of a year you've had." By the time she had finished she had left the guests feeling important and capable whether they were or not. But I felt sorry for her when she said to Lady Park Bedlow, "Good morning, you remember me, I'm Miss Sparkes. I'm pleased to see you looking well. They seem to be looking after you."

Mrs Blous was drenched from head to foot.

"Of course they are! If they didn't, I wouldn't stay here. I'm not a child," she snapped.

I felt sorry for Miss Sparkes. She didn't merit the reply, whereas Miss Dunne, our last nursing officer, did.

One little upsetting episode occurred due to the district nurse moving to another area, where she tells us she is to be a health visitor. She has spent one morning a week for the past 11 years bathing the few guests who can't manage to bath themselves. She is very good and I'm sure will make an excellent health visitor. However, Jim rang headquarters as a result of no nurse coming in for two weeks, during which time I did the bathing. He asked when the new nurse would be coming and he was told, "My nurses are too important to do dirty jobs like bathing old people!" He was furious.

"Would you put that in writing?" he asked, and hung up.

The phone rang 10 minutes later to inform him that the new nurse would call next week. She called all right! She took blind Mrs Hart to the bathroom and left her in the bath; rushed off to Mrs Lane, who couldn't get in the bath and, having washed her back and buttocks, she put the towel over her back and told her to dry herself, while she went upstairs to bath Miss Moss!

Mrs Hart's daughter stormed into the office before lunch. "Jim, Mummy's beside herself. Don't let that nurse near her again."

"What's happened?" said Jim.

"She left Mummy in the bath, told her to wash herself and that she would be back soon. Mr Findham walked into the bathroom. Mummy said, "Who's there?". He told her that she ought to be ashamed of herself for not locking the door. Mrs Lane had called Rose to dry her back where she could not reach."

"Don't worry. I heard her racing up the main staircase like a clumsy shire horse. I'll get someone to do the baths privately," said Jim. Now all is peaceful as Jenny's sister-in-law has taken on the job, and seems to enjoy it.

Too important to do dirty jobs like bath people! It's a good job I haven't taken that attitude when some guest has taken ill and needs constant washing and changing. Everybody's a General. There aren't any privates now.

We had a little party yesterday with all the guests and, later in the evening, with Peggy and Nobby. Mrs Raidell came down at 10 pm to enquire where her daughter was, and again said she would never give her daughter a silly name like Valerie.

"Have a sherry," said Jim, and she sat until midnight, pink cheeks getting shinier and shinier, and blue eyes twinkling.

Jim woke me up and asked me what I'd been dreaming.

"Oh, yes. I remember," I said. I'd written it down in the diary here. I was given two words with which to sign cheques or prescriptions, which a strange man said meant you never run out of money, or were cured instantly. I thought this will cure all the problems in the world. Let's see what the words were. Scrawled in large letters across the top of the diary were the words Bextire Bextilates!

Jim hasn't let me forget that one, or the night he said I woke him up shouting "Jim, Jim."

What's the matter?" he asked.

"You've shut yourself outside the front gate. Shall I go down and let you in?"

"No," he said and told me he'd wondered what would have

happened if he'd said "Yes." By lunch time the diary is half full. By the time I've continued to list events, the weather, the past, and menus, it is nearly full, then I finish it off before I go to sleep around midnight.

Jim dreamt that the telephone engineers demanded that the trees near the telephone pole were taken down. At 3 pm the phone went dead and at 4 pm the engineers arrived and said the trees were the cause of the trouble and we ought to get some taken down. I think Jim is changing his mind about precognition!

He is painting the library shelves. Mrs Raidell keeps coming to ask me who she is, and what she is doing here! I've just repapered Lady Parke Bedow's bathroom, and the handy man is building another chicken house.

Last week was a week I was glad to see the end of! As I walked into Major Twist's bedroom, which used to be the gun room in the olden days, I noticed that the parquet tiles were moving. It would cost a bomb to have the whole floor reset, so I would do it myself.

On Tuesday we left to buy fish and I showed our new staff member, a 50 year old very illiterate hospital inmate named Carry, the half-a-dozen blocks I wanted removed, and the space scrubbed. I should have known better! That was at 9.30 am. When I returned at 12.30 pm I nearly passed out with shock. She had removed over half the blocks in that 35 foot room!

I didn't know where to start. What had seemed easy with six spaces, seemed like a Chinese puzzle. I could have wept. However, donning a mac back to front, a hat, rubber boots, and rubber gloves, I collected a can of paraffin rags and black rubber mastic, and began after lunch. It was 11 pm before the Major could get to bed. That has taught me a lesson, I thought.

The next day Carry said, "I'll clean the oven."

"You'll do no such thing, Carry. Jenny cleans the Rayburn and the gas cooker every day. You forget it," I said.

At 9.30 that night I opened the lounge door to face a white paint bespattered Carry.

"It won't come off," she said.

"What won't come off?"

"The oven. I've been cleaning the oven and it won't come off," she repeated.

Dear God! She had taken a new two pint tin of gloss paint and wiped the oven out with it. I was frantic in case of fire. I stood with her until midnight. Hot water, detergents, scrapers and brushes were used until we got it all right.

"She'll have to go. We won't be able to sleep in case she does something else stupid," I said to Jim.

She'd had all her teeth out before she came to us and every day she had demanded something different to eat, using her lack of teeth as an excuse.

"Oh let her have what she wants," I'd said to Cook.

Every day she had also said, "The first thing I want to eat when I get teeth in, is salad. I love salad." And so, eventually, came the Saturday Carry had her teeth fitted.

On Sunday nights we serve the evening meal, leaving the staff's ready for them when they return from church. Carry was washing up when she suddenly turned to me and, pointing to the ham salad, said, "Ere, you don't expect me to eat that. That's rabbit's food. I want something else." I exploded.

"For two months we've heard nothing every day except that you can't wait to get your teeth to eat some salad. Well, if you don't eat it you can go without. You've played us up enough," I said, and I left the kitchen. I was furious as I related the conversation to Jim in the hall, but we were highly amused to hear Carry singing in a very high key, "There is a happy land, far far away, where they get ham and eggs, three times a day".

At 8.30 pm I went to the staff room and found Carry surrounded by fruit, chocolates, wine, beer and biscuits, telling the staff how we had starved her and how all the guests had taken pity on her, as she'd gone from room to room to tell them how badly she'd been treated. The day after this, her daughter collected her to take her home for the day to introduce her to the boy she was going to marry. Carry attacked the boy friend, so they rushed her back to hospital — for which we were truly grateful.

Jim bought two pairs of pure Irish linen sheets to fit our five foot bed. We had John and Alison to dinner and I left the table to see if a guest who was ill was comfortable. She was wet and, to save time, instead of going to the linen cupboard I took a new linen sheet from my bedroom and changed her. The next day I boiled three sheets, spun them, and put them on the airer to dry.

At 9 am the next morning all the staff were in the kitchen when I walked in, glanced up, and saw four sheets! I investigated the linen. One sheet had been neatly cut in half.

"Who did this?" I asked. There was silence. "One of you has cut this sheet in half. Come on, own up."

Mai's Norfolk accent rent the air. "Well, it's too big for a bed. Now you've got two sheets that fit the beds." I never answered, I walked out. Later I came upon Jenny talking to Rose in the linen room.

"Ee by gum I do feel sorry for you, I'd have let rip," said Jenny.

Rose tugged her hair upwards saying, "I'm only here for a few hours. If I was here all day I'd go crazy, I would never have your patience."

"It's all right Rose, I've recovered now," I said. The time I was really frustrated, was after I had run backwards and forwards four times a day to attend to Anne and Joan when they had 'flu. The first day they were back in the kitchen they said, "Sure and you know you owe us two days off. We'll be taking them all together with our day off this week."

I'll write once all the arrangements are made for the holiday.

Much love,
Lillian.

My dear Tilly,

Mr Palmer was 96 years of age yesterday and celebrated with a party in the evening, as well as with a tea party in the afternoon. He's very fit and normally maintains a reasonable conversation, commenting on the various items of news he reads in his morning paper, but last week we realised that he doesn't understand as much as he claims to. He said he would like an appointment to see the doctor because his skin irritated, so the appointment was made. The doctor's partner arrived to examine him and he had not met him before, but, apparently, as a young boy he knew the old man's father. After the examination he declared he couldn't find anything wrong, but would prescribe a cream. I left them in earnest conversation and, crossing the landing 10 minutes later, heard the doctor talking about the union NATSOPA, with whom apparently he didn't agree. On his way out he stopped to tell me what a remarkable man Mr Palmer was.

"He's got all his faculties, just like his father, whom I knew as a boy, and he can remember things that happened a few years ago that I can't remember," he said. "The cream will solve the problem. He's remarkably fit and, mentally, a truly remarkable man. Remarkable!" he continued, as he walked into the porch.

Five minutes later Mr Palmer approached me and said, "Tell me, this Nat Soper the doctor kept on about, is he any relation of Lord Soper?". I wouldn't dream of repeating this to the doctor, but we were amused and thought of the false impression one can get about people on first acquaintance.

Mrs Elliott, who's in her 90s, is not an academic but has become a first class business woman, a devout Christian with a sound knowledge of literature. Her ancestors were artists and I could spend hours listening to her. She sits quietly listening to everyone and rarely joins in a conversation, but when we are by ourselves she bubbles when I ask her to tell me about people and events she has found interesting. I'm entranced by the tales her mother, father and uncles told her about the lives of their parents when she was a child.

She told me she had acted when young in the play "The Monkey's Paw', in which an old couple had been given a monkey's paw with which they could make three wishes. They first wished for money, and the wish was swiftly granted when a man from the shipping office presented them with a sum of money together with condolences that their son had lost his life at sea. The second wish was that he should come home, and they heard him walking stiff and stilted with water dropping off him and knew his corpse had returned. They used the third wish to wish him back in his watery grave. To a modern generation this may seem old hat Tilly, but the moral behind the play still applies today. I do believe that when one wishes or prays for something good for other people one's prayers are answered, and if not, God knows best why they shouldn't be.

We have actually known of a most distressing case. A lady left her fortune to her niece, but only on the great niece's coming of age. The old lady died and the niece complained bitterly that she could have done with the money there and then.

"Why, oh why, did she have to arrange it this way?," she moaned to us. She got the money. Her only daughter committed suicide within a fortnight of the Aunt's death. No love or compassion was shown about the aunt dying; the only concern she had was the Aunt's money — and that brings me to another point. Euthanasia! If that should ever become law in any country you would find that old people would be wiped out like flies for money. Nobody has suffered with us. Our doctor has been superb by ensuring that no one has suffered pain while dying. The world's leaders and Royalty would be cossetted and kept going as long as possible, but billions of people like you and I would have a label attached to our records saying "Do not resuscitate".

The wise and humane country is the country that respects age and looks after its old people, and the disabled as well as children. I'm sure there are millions of people throughout America, Europe and the whole western World who are doing a marvellous job of looking after old people, much better than me, but I'm equally sure that as many old people are suffering from loneliness, which is the worst thing you can suffer from.

I must tell you about the funny dream I had. I went to bed with a terrible migraine and eventually fell asleep after Jim had put some ice in towels and held it on my head. I dreamt I went to Buckingham Palace and complained about the migraine to the Queen. She called in her surgeon who examined my head, and then said, "I can see what the trouble is. The top half of your face doesn't match the bottom half. I'll slice it off and match it together."

Dreams are delightful when they're not precognitive — they're so funny. Jim dreamt he bought a new car and he was so annoyed when he went to the garage to find that someone had stolen the headlights and a two foot square flint from inside the bonnet that provided the spark for the ignition.

You commented on the prices slowly increasing. You are right, and every now and again I read articles about inflation, and what to invest in to beat it, but I think that we cannot safeguard ourselves against all the effects of rampant inflation. One thing we do know for sure and that is that human nature will not change. There will always be good and bad people. Did you know, Tilly, that it was quite unsafe to walk from one inn to another or even visit the theatre around 1780? How sad that once again people are afraid to walk the streets at night! I do hope that all the people will know again the joy of walking freely and safely in the streets. Thank God for the Police. They have a most dangerous and difficult job, and thank God we're British, because I believe what the clever J. B. Priestley once wrote — that if every Englishman did nothing for two years, the world would still owe them a living. Of course there have been bad Englishmen, as there are bad in all nationalities, but the good that has been done for, and in, other countries is quickly forgotten — as the appalling custom of suttee has been forgotten, where an Indian wife was burnt to death on the husband's pyre. This was stopped as a result of the British Raj in India.

Look forward to your news.

Much love,
Lillian.

2nd OCTOBER, 1966

Tilly dear,

It made an hilarious evening for Jim when I repeated our conversation on the phone. The next day we had an hilarious time here. I disguised myself as an old man after going through a box of fancy dress we have in the attic. I borrowed one of the gentlemen's coats and a trilby hat, men's shoes, false nose, dark glasses, a beard and gloves, and walked into the kitchen dressed thus for a joke. When they finished laughing, Jenny suggested that I went and sat in the lounge. Most of the guests were in there and I got Anne to lead me to a chair and say, "This is the new guest, Mr Jones."

Oh dear, Tilly, it was funny to hear the remarks. Several spoke to me, and I nodded and cupped my ear with a gloved hand, making out I was deaf. Comments were made like, "Poor old man, I think he's deaf," and "Not very talkative, is he?".

Mr Banks moved next to me as Mrs Mainwaring left the chair.

"Come for a trial period have you?" he asked.

I nodded.

"They always tell you that, but you're stuck here for good now. Got any family?"

I shook my head.

"Do you watch the television?"

I nodded.

"You don't have much to say for yourself do you?"

I shook my head.

"That's a relief. Banks talks enough. We don't want two of them," I heard the Major say quietly to Mr McGregor. I stood up and removed the disguise and all but a couple of guests had a good laugh.

It was Bank Holiday madness that must have affected me, because I remembered that months before, John and Alison had come to dinner after listening to an argument between Jim and I over the merits of buying a deep freeze. He wanted one, I didn't. We received a phone call the following night from a man who sounded like a cockney.

He said, "Look 'ere lady. I've arrived in the village with this 'ere deep freezer of yours. Can you give me directions to the house?" I argued with him for several minutes stating that I hadn't ordered it and wasn't going to have it. He began to laugh and I recognized John's voice. He'd been pulling my leg, posing as a cockney driver.

"We must return the joke one day," I said to Jim, but forgot about it until, leaving the lounge to replace the clothes I'd borrowed, I met our neighbour's daughter and her American husband. They were coming in to have tea with us.

Peter Conte, a tall handsome Texan with a nice deep Southern American accent, was discussing life in America when I interrupted to ask them to come back in the evening and join our two friends John and Alison who were coming to dinner that night. They agreed, and I recalled the deep freezer episode.

"John is in advertising. I've got it! With your accent you can phone him and tell him you want him to handle the advertising on this side of the Atlantic for a new idea your firm has developed in the States."

I got the writing pad out and worked for five minutes, and handed it with the phone number to Peter Conte. He phoned John, informed him that he'd been trying to get hold of him for days but was due to fly to America the next day, and wanted him to handle the advertising of this wonderful idea that had proved so successful in America.

"Women love colour, Mr Bear, and by introducing colour into fish, we've increased sales 500 per cent in the States. We have pink plaice, green bream, lemon sole. You name the fish and we've got a colour for it."

For five minutes the conversation continued till eventually he said, "As I have to fly back tomorrow Mr Bear, I'm going to hand you over to my Scottish agent, Angus McCreep."

Jim took the phone and, in a marvellous Scottish accent, said, "Do ye no ken the idea of a purple haddie?". We all drowned the next remark with laughter. Later that evening, while having dinner, John described his emotions on hearing Peter. He'd thought, "Trust these Americans to phone on a Bank Holiday and expect one to jump to the idea straight away". It was a warm, lovely, happy atmosphere. The best entertainment is always home made.

The day after this was an eventful one. Mrs Mainwaring, who likes walking four or five miles a day, never returned for lunch. After an hour's driving round looking for her Jim phoned the police. After four hours we'd had no lunch and we were desperate. We had phoned her son and informed him. At 9.15 pm we received a phone call to inform us that the police were on their way back with her. Apparently she'd got lost and forgotten her name. Seeing a queue of women, she joined it and found herself in a factory on the night shift. She looks more like a 60-year-old than 70 odd. When they realised that she wasn't on the payroll, they phoned the police. Then they gave her a meal in the canteen while waiting for the police. Jim gave them a contribution to the police fund and we were very relieved to see her back.

Dear Mai is knitting away furiously. Actually, she's an expert when it comes to knitting, and each Christmas she presents each lady with a pair of bedsocks and each gentleman with a pair of ordinary socks. Rose said to her, "You make us look mean as we only give flowers and chocolates to be shared."

Mai said, "You do what you like. These have been the happiest years of my life."

Yesterday I was annoyed when Mary, who is not very bright, asked Mai for a cloth to dry off the corridor she was scrubbing. I stepped into the corridor and saw Mary drying it with a new bathmat; price 35 shillings.

"Mary, what are you doing? Where did you get that?" I asked.

"Mai gave it to me. She took it out of the linen cupboard and said, 'That will dry it for you'." I gave her fresh floor cloths and took the soiled bathmat to Mai and asked her why she gave it to Mary.

"That's all right. That don't matter," drawled Mai slowly, in her Norfolk dumpling accent.

"It matters very much. Another time send Mary to me. If it happens again I'll have to ask Rose to lock the linen cupboard, and I don't want to do that." Leaving the kitchen I heard Mai say, "Missus is all right, but I don't take no notice of her."

The next morning I popped my head into Mrs Hart's room to tell Rose that it was time for a break. I found her on her hands and knees polishing the surrounds, with the bed and wardrobe moved to the centre of the room. Through the adjoining door we heard Lady Lyle saying, "I don't think Rose ever cleans my room. When Mrs Martin visited me yesterday she said, 'Look under your dressing table. There's a safety pin on the floor, that was there a fortnight ago.' I quite believe that she comes into my room for five minutes when she arrives, but I've never seen her clean the room nor the furniture yet".

Rose stood up, gripped her hair, and pulled it saying, "What do you do with them?"

"Calm down Rose, let me tell you what happened yesterday," I said, and told her about the bathmat. After listening she said, "Well it isn't so bad for me as I can get away from it all."

Dear Rose, she leaves with a shopping list from various guests every lunchtime, although Jim and I get their shopping. Anne, Jenny and Mai also bring back shopping for the guests, plus their relations and friends.

It's time I made sure that everyone is comfortably tucked up, so once again I'll say goodnight. I'll phone on Monday night.

Much love,
Lillian.

Dear Tilly,

We feel sad because two guests have passed over — Miss Lock, whom I nursed till the end, and Mr James, who had to be removed to hospital. Mr James weighed 17 stone. The doctor sent a district nurse to help me.

She gave one look at him and said, "Certainly not. He needs a man to lift him."

I phoned the surgery and a second nurse came.

"Oh no, he needs a man. I'll report back," she said.

After tea a male nurse arrived, looked at Mr James and then asked me if I had a phone. I took him to the office where he explained on the phone that it would be physically impossible to lift him without two strong men and probably some weight lifting equipment. Mr James was taken to hospital that night and died two days later.

I miss those two guests. They always found good in everyone and in everything that was done for them. Mr James was a scientist — silent and wise. If he hadn't been crippled by arthritis he would not have been with us. In the winter he played cards a lot and I often stopped to play for an hour with him, he was such good company.

Two new guests have taken their places, a Colonel Yates and a Mr Bellows. Mr Bellows was a gardener in the same job for nearly 50 years and his employer left him a large sum of money. During his second week here we heard a crash and rushed to investigate. In the dash I caught my foot in something and found myself flat on my face with Jim on top of me. We were enmeshed with springs. Somebody had stupidly come back from the bathroom and switched off the lights in the bathroom. Mr Bellows, feeling for the light switch with one hand, had put his other hand on the catch of one of two folding beds we keep folded up in the bathroom in case of emergency, and it had crashed open. I was all blood and bruises, but Jim and Mr Bellows were all right. A week later he got an attack of 'flu. I called in the doctor and he was put on antibiotics.

A week later he was as fit as a fiddle, and I said, "You can get up now Mr Bellows."

"No, I'm not, I'm too old. I'm going to stay in bed and be waited on." He got out of bed and moved to the commode.

"Oh come, Mr Bellows, I'll take you to the bathroom," I said, and I escorted him there, and returned to make his bed and help him dress when he'd finished. He came back, but insisted on getting into bed, so

I arranged for the doctor to see him. Mai came into the room and asked if I'd seen what was in the bathroom. Mr Bellows had used the bath to defecate instead of the toilet! The doctor arrived and told him he needed exercise and that he was fit.

The next morning he both wet the bed and defecated in it, and when I entered the room he said, "See that? I'll do it again if you try to make me leave this room." I phoned his solicitor and arranged a transfer to a nursing home, as I could see he had become "gaga".

His niece visited him with a friend that afternoon, and I could hear her telling the friend on the way out that she was going to report us as the poor old uncle had said he'd not been given a bite of food since he came in! Poor man; but what about the relative who has somebody like that on their own to look after? Anyway, a Miss Scott has moved into his room and seems happy.

Colonel Yates has settled down and has been made a great fuss of by the ladies. He has a taxi once a week to take him to his club in the West End, and he invited me to go and have dinner with him. I enjoyed it very much. It gave me the opportunity to do a couple of hours shopping and join him at the club later.

This brings to mind an incident that occurred three weeks ago. He'd asked Jim if he would look after a magnificent gold watch which he said he wanted to get repaired. Jim locked it in the office drawer and a few days later he asked for it back. One week later, as he was ready to set off to London, he asked Jim for the gold watch.

"I've given it back to you," said Jim.

"No, I haven't got it."

"I assure you you have," said Jim.

The Colonel got red in the face and was quite tetchy when I suggested that I look in his pockets. He left eventually and I began to search his room. I didn't search it once. I searched over and over again. I was beside myself with worry, as I knew the staff wouldn't have touched it, but I remembered that, the day before, the telephone engineers were in and out of the hall. The Colonel's door was always open and it would have been possible to remove anything from the room unnoticed. Five minutes before lunch I went into the office and prayed. I prayed as I have never prayed that the watch would be found. As I left the office the phone rang. It was the waiter from the club in London. He said the Colonel said he wished to apologise. He was having lunch with his son, who had just given him back the watch he had taken away for repair last week. So our prayers *do* get answered, and there was a happy end to the problem.

If we were to tell that story to some people they would say that he forgot because he was old, but that is not the case at all. Have you noticed what people say when young people forget, or swear they did

56

something when they have forgotten to do it? They always say they've got too much on their minds. Recently a bright 18-year-old promised three days running to pop back with a book his father wished to lend us. He apologised each time and said he forgot as soon as he got back, as he had so many other things he was trying to remember.

The other night we were all laughing and joking about who we'd like to be marooned on a desert island with. Mostly the guests mentioned people they liked to watch on television. A few said they couldn't think of anyone. Two ladies said Jim, and Mr Shalk said me, because he thought he'd be sure of a dinner. Later by ourselves, we talked about the merriment that the question produced, but after listing all the friends we have, there were less than half a dozen we'd fancy being marooned with, because most of our academic friends failed hopelessly when it came to listing their capabilities in the practical field, much as we love them.

I've often talked to you about Helen, who is truthful, honest, utterly charming, brilliant at languages and with a first class degree. Well the other evening we talked for an hour on the phone and the conversation began with her request for advice as to whether she should buy a fridge-freezer or a fridge and a freezer, as she thought it was time to replace her fridge. We discussed other subjects, but kept coming back to the question of the fridge. Eventually I said, "It's got to be a fridge-freezer."

"But there must be an advantage one way or the other," she said.

"What do you mean? What kind of advantage?" I asked.

"Well supposing there was a power cut. At least you'd have one working."

Tilly, I couldn't believe my ears; now you see what I mean about thinking carefully who you'd choose to be on a desert island with. With Helen one would never be without conversation or amusement, but when it came to finding a meal or making a shelter, one would have to be prepared to work hard.

It will soon be time to say all my goodnights.

Look forward to your news.

Much love,
Lillian.

20th JANUARY, 1967

Dear Tilly,

I'm exhausted. The unbelievable has occurred. Jim's brother, a scientist who lives in America, is over here on holiday with us, and we gave him the first of four rooms in the four-roomed flat leading off the main building. The room at the other end, a very large one with large double doors leading on to the lawn and a window on either side, is occupied by Mrs James. Next to her is Anne and the other is occupied by the cook.

At 1.30 am the other morning, we were woken by an urgent knocking on the door. It was the cook.

"Mrs James has been attacked by a man," she said, white-faced and shaking. Grabbing my dressing gown I fled down stairs with Jim, who was checking his watch for the time. Bruce stood at the bottom of the staircase and said, "It's all right, I've rung the police."

I found Mrs James, white and shaken, sitting in a chair by the corridor door. I examined her and found her pulse to be over a hundred, and thready. I assured her that she would be all right, and that we would carry her into the main building, bath her and put her back to bed. Then, having observed the evidence of blood and semen on her nightdress, I asked, "What happened?"

"I heard a sound outside the window, switched on my bedside light and saw a young man who was standing on the sill, with his head looking over the top of the sill. 'Don't I know you? Can I help you?' I said. Then he pushed the window down, climbed over it, put the light out and got into bed with me. I'd looked at the time. It was a quarter to one. Eventually he said, 'Tell me where the girls sleep or I'll murder you.' So I told him they slept in the next two rooms. He left me and then I heard Anne screaming."

I called Anne and cook into the room and told them to sit with Mrs James while I got them all something to drink. I laced the milk with brandy and poured fresh tea into the cups and handed it to the three of them, and listened to Anne babbling of how she woke up, switched the light on and saw this face within a few inches of her nose. She screamed non-stop. He flung the window up and rushed away through it.

There was a tap on the door. I went into the corridor. It was the local policeman, Joe Harris. After I had given him their versions he said, "Are you sure she was raped?"

"Yes, I can let you have the evidence after I've bathed her."

Right, I'll go and phone the doctor," he said.

"Just a minute. She doesn't have our doctor," I said, "She has her own. I'll give you the phone number and wait for you to come back."

As I waited with Mrs James and the girls, I listened to adamant protestations that they would never sleep in the flat again.

"Well, stop worrying. We'll carry the mattresses over for you and make you comfortable for the night in the staff room," I assured them. Joe Harris came back and I stripped their beds, and Jim helped me to carry the mattresses over and make the two beds up.

I was about to walk back to the flat when I heard a man's angry voice shouting, "What the bloody hell is going on here?". It was a 50-year-old Dr Vance, who was standing in for her own doctor who was on holiday. We walked back to the flat. Jim took the girls back to the staff room. By now both drives were stiff with police and tracker dogs. The doctor sat down, looked at the tea cups and shouted, "What's this? I didn't expect to be called out to a bloody tea party." It was unbelievable!

I explained what had happened. He took her pulse and said, "There's nothing the matter with you. You bloody well enjoyed it." Tilly, can you imagine how I felt? Poor Mrs James sat there speechless!

Dr Vance left and I stepped into the corridor. Joe Harris had heard every word.

"What's the matter with him?" he asked. I told him exactly what had happened, adding that he was a rude, drunken, uncaring lout.

"I thought I had misheard him at first, but she must be examined. I'll have to phone for the police surgeon. He duly arrived, examined her and confirmed that she had been raped. Then we took her over to the main building, where I bathed her and put her to bed.

That was not the end of it. The detectives arrived and questioned her. Then a woman detective questioned her by herself for half an hour. Bruce was in the grounds helping to search for the young man who had been described as about 19 years of age. Jim was kept busy answering questions about any likely types he might have spotted in the area and also questions about Mrs James.

By 3 am I could have dropped, but I was asked to question her by myself, as they said she probably trusted me, and might give further clues about the young man's identity. Except that he had soft hands and didn't seem as if he had done any manual work, I got nowhere, so I told her to try and sleep, and insisted that she had a sleeping pill before I left her.

I made tea for the detectives. I was glad of a cup myself by this time. Then it dawned on me. What about the other guests? They might panic. What could we do to prevent them knowing? We decided to warn the staff not to discuss it with the guests and I said to Jim, "I'm going to London tomorrow. We must arrange for an intercom system to be fixed in every room — not that it would help in this type of case where the rapist is asked, "Do I know you? Can I help you?". He would probably overwhelm the guest before they pulled the switch.

The next day brought professional artists, more police, more detectives, and more worries as the news had got out. The police had a word with the local newspaper editors, and they promised not to publish the name of either the house or guest. They kept their word but we were mad when we saw the evening paper and found it was full of a lot of nonsense about a rapist attacking a paralysed guest, who managed to drag herself along the floor to get help.

Mrs James said a young man from the newspaper had interviewed her for an hour. Nobody appears to have seen him. How he got to her room we can't understand, but someone must have shown him to it. Jim rang the editor and protested. I caught the cook going to her room with a hammer "to protect herself" as she put it. Altogether we were kept on our feet for 23 hours and I didn't get to London until the next day.

Within a few weeks every room will have an intercom service, and thank goodness, the guests have calmed down. Mrs James was adamant and didn't believe that lightning struck twice, so we gave in. The cook has stopped marching backwards and forwards with a hammer, too.

As you can see life hasn't been funny, but my sense of humour was restored yesterday, when I overheard Mrs Hart say to Mr McGregor, who seems to have got much deafer. "I think I've lost a couple of pounds with worry. My skirt has got slacker."

"What's that about crackers?"

"I said my skirt has got slacker."

"What have I done with my cracker?"

"No, no, my skirt has got slacker".

He just shook his head and walked off.

We have a new guest, an 84-year-old Major Miles. I introduced him to 96-year-old Mr Shalk and Mr Howe. As I walked off I heard Mr Howe say to Mr Shalk, "He makes you look a youngster!"

"Oh no," I thought. How tactless.

I do look forward to your letters. Hurry up and write.

Love,
Lillian.

Tilly my dear,

No hope of getting a holiday this year, but never mind. Every room in the house is filled with sweet peas; the faster we cut them the more there are. We're surprised to hear from you that the farmer has uprooted the hedge at the top of the bank in front of your house, and taken all the trees down. That will not only alter the outlook, but will result in your feeling the winds more from that direction I would think. On fine days all guests have been sitting out on the lawn, and the staff out there with them. Everything was fine, except for one unexpected event.

You remember I told you about one of the guests getting raped and that they never did catch the young man. Well, the other evening a man of about 40, a nondescript type of character, rang the bell at 7.30 pm. He asked to see the owner and I told him he was addressing the owner. He proceeded to tell me that he had information that I might wish to take advantage of as, on the night a rape was committed here, he was at a party in the village. He had seen a young man at the party who left at 11.30 pm but had seen him coming back at 1.30 am and knew the young man had committed the act of rape on a number of occasions. He said he didn't want to get involved.

I said, "Excuse me, I'm wanted in the kitchen. Please step inside a minute." I escorted him to the lounge and said to Jim, "This gentleman has some information for you."

I ran to the office, rang Joe Harris, our local constable, and reported the conversation. He arrived within four minutes, followed by more policeman who took the man to the police station. Joe Harris told us that he'd been suspected of another rape and had named the boy to try and throw the blame. The deviousness of people, Tilly.

I had to smile after the builder finished the repairs to the roof, which he does annually. While settling the bill in the office, he told me that he'd had a very salutory lesson when he was younger. After doing repairs in the house of a young married woman, he presented the bill and the young lady, according to him, asked him to come up into the bedroom to estimate how much the decoration would cost. He said he spent 20 minutes up there examining the rooms before giving her a price, while her daughter was downstairs crayoning in a book. When she came down she told him she'd paid the bill as he'd been allowed to come up into the bedroom, and the child could prove that he came up the stairs! How much of this was true I don't know, but I thought it would amuse you.

A window cleaner once told me that he wouldn't have made any money if he'd accepted all the proposals he'd had of paying him off in bed. I didn't believe him, but as I see the Western World becoming more and more permissive I think there may have been a grain of truth in it. How awfully sad that women could think so little of themselves. I think that the situation has far surpassed anything that Huxley or Orwell imagined, and the people who will suffer most in the end will be women. It was right to fight for freedom. Now they fight for licence.

What produced these thoughts was probably that when Mrs Hart's daughter was talking to half-a-dozen of her mother's friends over a drink the other morning, she told them that her friend in St John's Wood had been burgled twice in a year, and how ghastly it had been for her. What *was* ghastly was poor Mai's sister being broken into twice in one year, and the second time they kicked and wrecked every piece of furniture and every wardrobe that she'd polished with pride for 40 years. Each of the guests had stories to tell of friends or relatives who had been mugged or had their homes broken into.

I left the room to be greeted by Mr Muir's daughter, a left wing academic, who is absolutely charming. I remarked on the conversation we'd just had. She said that people died in the 30s of TB as a result of being able only to afford bread and margarine. Rubbish! I was a teenager when war broke out, and working for my living. She had just left Oxford with a degree, and lived abroad. Rich people died of TB as well as poor people. TB was very infectious and living in damp houses or getting soaking wet on a job all day contributed to many poor people succumbing to it.

She said that the poorest people in this country were rich beyond the dreams of avarice in comparison to most of the Third World countries, and that today they don't have to be put away in mental hospitals because they're expecting a baby. She said the poorest people were now secure and had the freedom to enjoy sex without being thought of as wanton.

"Whoever told you that girls were put into mental hospitals if they got pregnant?" I asked her. As you know, Tilly, that's a lot of left-wing propaganda that she's been listening to. Most of them got married and those that couldn't get married were all right if they had loving parents. Those that didn't filled the Barnados, Nazareth and other homes. Many had their babies adopted. The few that were thrown out and ended in the workhouse stayed there until their children were weaned, and were then found a job. If they didn't help to support the child out of their wages then they usually signed it away for adoption. Of course, the odd girl might have gone into a mental hospital, but because she suffered from a mental illness, *not* because she was pregnant.

"If the poor are so affluent, how do you account for the fact the people in the country can no longer leave their doors open at night, which was the custom for many country people even as late as the mid-1950s?" I asked.

"Oh, there have always been no-go areas in cities," she replied.

"That wasn't the question. Of course there were parts of cities where people only went if they were crooked, or seeking some unlawful excitements, but we enjoyed walking the streets without fear of getting mugged, and, as I said, in the country many people didn't lock the door. We didn't, but now people are afraid to live alone."

Everything is condoned, not condemned. They are destroying everything that's beautiful and good, and civilisation is breaking up.

Oh well, we just have to pray and hope that common sense will prevail and that good will overcome evil.

Will phone on Sunday.

Much love,
Lillian.

Tilly dear,

We were surprised to read that the headmaster said to your daughter that it wasn't important if she wasn't making progress in her reading, but that it was good she could swim.

I liked your answer; "It is important, and you never taught her to swim. Her grandfather taught her." I can see how mad she was when she saw that the teacher had corrected the spelling from "Balon" to "baloon" instead of "balloon". You're quite right; we deprive children if we don't get them interested in books as early as possible.

One of my guests, who was a teacher, said that when she was young only a tiny number of children left school incapable of writing their names. The guest to whom she was talking said that her 12-year-old grandchild was skilled in punching out the answer on a computer, but couldn't work out arithmetic on paper or spell correctly. A gentleman guest joined in by telling them that the child who can read among a group of illiterates is like a one-eyed king in the country of the blind. This was followed by a political argument about which government had been to blame for letting this state of affairs come about. I won't bore you with the remarks. You can well imagine them — some sensible and some silly came from both camps.

Each guest brings either joy or a problem, so I will now tell you about Mrs Gwendolyn Ross Hewitt. She arrived here 12 months ago — 80 years of age; fussy, immaculate, and talkative. She had two sons, both in very highly paid positions which involved travelling. We discovered she was very light-fingered, but we didn't worry, as when things went missing, such as jewellery, a search of her room always produced the missing article which could then be restored to its owner. During the eight months she was with us, every time she received post cards from abroad she painstakingly peeled off the back from each card — perfectly. We couldn't understand why she should do this until I overheard Mr McGregor say to her, "You ought to report them to the police."

I asked him what she should report. He said, "The notes that her son always seals between the view and the card." I told him that the idea was ridiculous, but it set us thinking about the possibilities of her unsealing other people's letters during her lifetime.

Two months ago she became quite crazy. I rang the son who'd arranged for her to stay here and he pleaded with me to keep her, as he said his brother had been rushed to hospital with a mental breakdown two nights before. I agreed under the circumstances, but thought it odd because she couldn't stop talking about the son who'd had the breakdown for two days. She kept saying "I must go to him," although she could not have heard from anyone about this. I did wonder from then on if she was also psychic.

The son came out of hospital and went abroad with his wife on a holiday and I found that the staff or myself had to follow Mrs Hewitt round, as she had developed a habit of stripping off stark naked in front of the window before trying to balance her clothes on her head. The big worry was that she'd start to do this in front of the guests and I'd have to rush in to prevent her removing the lot, and dress her again! Eventually her son and daughter-in-law returned from holiday and he went abroad again. The situation became desperate so I rang the daughter-in-law and asked her to make arrangements to move her mother-in-law to either a psychiatric nursing home or a nursing home.

"It will have to wait until my brother-in-law comes home. I'm full up with guests now," she said.

Tilly, was I angry! We'd looked after her without charging nursing fees and it transpired that the daughter-in-law was running a nice little tax-free business charging nearly three times what we charged, and not being registered as a business or paying business rates or other overheads, while her husband was earning a fortune in his job.

"You must remove her today or pay nursing home fees," I said, naming a figure six times the amount she was paying and equivalent to a top nursing home fee.

She arrived within two hours and took her to a nursing home where the fees were two and a half times what she paid us and, in the circumstances, the staff at the nursing home would have earned every penny.

This week one of the villagers visited an aunt in the same nursing home as Mrs Hewitt and told me that she's drugged up a bit now as she caused chaos by telling the patients that she owned the nursing home, that the owner was her husband and that they must do as she said. Apparently the owners and staff had been very good to her but had had to use drugs to quieten her so the other patients could get some peace. One can always feel sorry for the Mrs Hewitts who live in a fantasy world, but you get mad when you find that people are not straight with you. We did them a favour out of sympathy because of the son's illness, and they should have been straight and removed her as soon as they came back from their holiday.

Jim bought Peter Pug for me a couple of months ago. Of course all the guests spoil him. He knows he has got them all under his paw. I had a surprise the day after Mrs Hewitt left. Nobody has ever given me money and I've never expected it, so you can imagine how I felt when I went upstairs to get a rest at 3 pm, feeling a little depressed, when Anne brought me a cup of tea at 4 pm with a letter from Mrs Hook. It said that she'd often wondered how she could repay me for looking after her during the last four years and, now that she'd found out what Peter cost, would I accept the cheque inside to pay for him as he gave joy to her and others besides ourselves. I was over the moon as you can imagine. Peter's large brown eyes bewitch all the guests and gentle Silvy, the spaniel mothers him. I let Mai have him for a couple of hours in the night in the staffroom because she's so crazy about him.

I was walking back down the drive yesterday when a strange voice said, "What's your rush, Ginger?" I never looked back. It was the new milkman! When I went into the kitchen this morning he was talking to cook. She asked me if I wanted to order any cream and introduced me. His face went red as I smiled at him. Oh well, its flattering to know that a back view still produces interest. Three or four times as Jim has caught up with me today he's said, "What's your rush, Ginger?".

The house is overheated and I heard two guests dressed in summer dresses say, "Isn't it cold today?" and I thought of how lucky we all are — especially when you think of what it was like for people in the years 1683, 1709, 1715, 1739, 1767, 1788 and 1814, when the cold was "so great that the smoke couldn't rise, so that the lungs were filled with gross particles, exceedingly obstructing the breathing". In 1739 many people who had lived in Hudson's Bay territory, declared that they had never known it colder in that frozen region than England was during that winter. Vessels laden with corn, coal, etc., were sunk by ice and many people lost their lives due to the severity of the weather.

"The hand of charity was liberally extended. Great benefactions were given by people of oppulent fortunes. Considerable collections were made in each parish. Many families living in a wretched state were preserved as a result". I've quoted here from that fascinating book, *Old and New London.*

In this century, 1947 and 1963 were severe winters, but due to an improvement in transport and living conditions, although some lives were lost due to hypothermia, most people were able to combat the worst of it.

It's usually the people who suffer the most who complain the least, but, thank God, due to some scientific discoveries and caring doctors, it's not necessary for people to die in agony today; yet the quicker we find cures for physical ailments the more people suffer from mental ailments. The cure for most of today's type of mental illness is in loving and doing for people, as Christ and his disciples pointed out. Alas, the most inadequate and incapable people are now encouraged to consider themselves too important to do menial tasks, and those that appeared adequate and capable often become mentally ill due to utter selfishness.

We have some consolation in the fact that there are people who share our views on the great moral issues of the day such as Mary Whitehouse, John Junor, Malcolm Muggeridge and others. Millions share their views, but are not heard because it's only informed public opinion that's taken notice of. Thank God they are brave enough to speak for us lesser mortals.

It's time for me to say "goodnight" to everyone. When I've finished I'll sit with Jim, Silvy, Peter and Redvers and drink a toast to you. I know Redvers is a male parrot — he kisses my cheeks non-stop, but lunges at Jim if he attempts to kiss me.

Much love,
Lillian.

My dear Friend,

What a delightful letter! I enjoyed your funny dream. I hope the one I had last night doesn't come true. I dreamt it was midnight and I was dialling 999 for the police, as there was a huge fire on the lawn in front of my bedroom window.

The reason I didn't write was because we went on holiday and Jim became very ill. Peggy and her husband took over for us and I arranged for extra help so that we could spend a week in Cornwall. We were over the moon to be able to get away for a week, but read on and tell me what you think in your next letter.

We left at seven o'clock in the morning and had arranged for a taxi to meet us at five o'clock, at the end of the journey, to take us to our hotel. Jim just toyed with his lunch and by four o'clock looked quite flushed. He complained of feeling hot. We arrived at the hotel, bathed, changed and came down to dinner, but he couldn't eat it although it was tasty and attractive, and said he needed fresh air.

The next morning he said "I'll be alright if I can get out in the fresh air. I'll take you to Penzance."

We arrived in Penzance and asked a policeman to recommend a good hotel for lunch, but when it arrived he apologised and said he couldn't eat it, so I excused myself rushed out to a chemist and bought a thermometer. It registered 105!!

We got back to the hotel and I asked the receptionist to phone the doctor. The manageress approached me and said we couldn't have the doctor. We would have to visit him. I stormed, and the doctor arrived. He was young and kind. He came every day, but Jim's temperature stayed up. He admitted he didn't know what was wrong, but thought maybe he had a secondary infection. I cancelled our seats and booked sleeping berths as we had to get back by the Sunday. Nobby was due back to work on Monday. He manages an electrical shop.

I paid the hotel bill. They charged me £1.00 per day extra for bringing iced orange up daily, and serving my lunch and breakfast in the room, and Jim hadn't had one meal. Neither had the manageress come near us!

We settled down in the sleeping berths when Jim said, "I smell gas." He staggered into the corridor, and we found the gas taps full on and unlit in the little room next to us. We put them off, but we were too frightened to sleep after that.

We arrived in London at 8 am. I hurriedly got a taxi and got Jim into it. After we'd been 15 minutes in the taxi, I remembered I had left my glasses in the train! When we arrived home I quickly got Jim to bed, phoned the doctor, explained the situation and asked if he would call the next morning.

Peggy and Nobby expressed great worry because they said it looked as though someone with giant rubber boots had been walking up and down during the night, churning the lawn up.

. . .it looked as though someone with giant rubber boots had been churning the lawn up.

"Stop worrying, it's not important. All that matters is that Jim gets well."

Eventually, to please them, I went out to have a look. "Oh, no, my God. Jim will have a heart attack if he sees this. There must have been at least 50 cattle here all night!" I thought.

I phoned the farmer's wife who said, "You don't worry about things like that when you get to my age. They broke out and some were found on the M1." The next morning the farmer and his son came to see me.

"What have you got on your mind? Damages? You should have fenced the place so that they couldn't get in," he said forbiddingly.

"The place is fenced with hedges. They broke through. I don't want damages, but it costs a fortune to keep this lawn perfect. My husband is very ill and can't put it right, so I'm asking you to put it right."

"Very well show us where the roller and the rake is, and we'll put it right," he said.

When I went upstairs Jim said, "I heard Old Farmer Wile's voice. What have you done to charm him?" I explained what had happened and said I hadn't wanted to worry him. He laughed.

"Don't be silly, I looked out of the bathroom window yesterday and saw what had happened, but I didn't mention it because I didn't want to worry *you*," he said.

Then the doctor arrived. Half an hour later he asked me if I would like to take a phial of Jim's blood to the hospital so that he could get the results quickly. He would call back.

He came in the evening and told Jim he had glandular fever.

"I might not have thought of it, but for the first time in years I had two cases recently," he said. "You'll get over it, but you must stay in bed, and I'm afraid it's one of those things where you will probably feel even worse for a little while when you're able to get up."

A week later we had that boiling hot weather. I walked into the bedroom. The windows were wide open and Jim just had a sheet on him. I've never seen anyone get out of bed as quick in my life. "Jim, I just saw a bee fly in under that sheet," I said. After the bee was set free we sat back and laughed.

Peggy and Nobby looked after everyone marvellously. They were liked by everyone, but she had been very worried in case anyone became ill. They felt so sorry for our spaniel, Tilly, that they allowed her to sleep on the bed in case she pined for us! She's back in her chair now.

The other big worry they had was due to a guest who has been here four years and claimed that the extra member of staff we took on had stolen her silver. The guest, a Miss Powell, had her nephew visit her the day after we left on holiday, and he went to the police and demanded that the girl's house was searched! The police spoke to Peggy and she phoned me.

"Certainly not, I'm always finding jewellery that she says has been taken. I'll find it when I come back I'm sure," I told Peggy.

Miss Powell had been packing up to leave the day the nephew called on her. She had been on holiday and met a nurse and her mother who said they loved old people, and if they had the money they knew of a home they would like to buy to look after old people. Miss Powell bought it for them! She gave us notice and then changed her mind about leaving. She showed me the letter they sent her back, telling her that they had been depending on looking after her to enable them to pay her back, so again she changed her mind.

I went through the tea chests and found her silver, and she apologised, then told me that it wouldn't have mattered if the girl's house had been searched by the police, as if the fact that her conscience was clear was all that mattered! What do you say to someone as stupid as Miss Powell? The poor girl's good name would have gone.

Anyway, poor Miss Powell made an awful mistake. She took our nice 95-year-old Miss Rice on a holiday with her when she moved out. Miss Rice wrote to me and gave notice, and a week later wrote and asked me to have her back. She said it was a mistake. There wasn't any heating or any guests. The house was old and full of dry rot and damp. She told Miss Powell she was coming back, and Miss Powell had a heart attack and died in front of her. Miss Powell's other nephew came to see us and said, "My aunt made a terrible mistake. If you saw the house you would be horrified. It needs as much spending on it as she paid for it, and they will never have the money to do it."

That's life, Tilly, as you know, more than I do. You've had more experiences of people's follies than I have.

I hope I'm writing something cheerful next time.

Love to all,
Lillian.

25th NOVEMBER, 1967

My dear Tilly,

Anne came back from Rome and excitedly showed the post cards to the staff. Later, Jenny said to me, "Did you see that picture of the Colla-something?"

"You mean the Colosseum," I replied.

"Ee, by gum. You'd have thought they would have spent some money on re-roofing it," she said.

We were speechless! Later, discussing it, we came to the conclusion that we'd be amazed if we could read the minds of half of the tourists in the world who travel to other countries on sightseeing tours.

A few weeks ago the social worker brought us a pretty 24-year-old girl named Cath Dollen. She seemed personable and capable, but when the social worker handed me her tablets, and I looked at the list, I had misgivings. It read — Chlorprom 100 mg 2 per day, Doxepin 25 mg 3 per day, Stellazin Trifluoperazine 5 mg 2 tabs three times per day, Benztropine 2 mg 1 tab three times per day, Nitrazepam 5 mg 2 tabs at night.

She assured me that Cath shouldn't be any trouble, and that the drugs kept her from relapsing into a state of suicidal tendency. All went well for about 10 days and then I woke up one morning and thought I heard faint screams in the distance. I rushed to investigate. It was 6.30 am. I found Anne crying in a corner of the kitchen between the Aga and the office window, and Cath Dollen screaming and bashing the Aga with a saucepan. I was terrified as well as Anne, but spoke quietly as though there wasn't anything wrong.

"I do understand how you feel Cath. Let me sit you down and give you a cup of tea."

I got the saucepan away from her and managed to get her seated, and then asked them what they were doing in the kitchen at 6.30 am instead of 7.30 am.

Cath said she hated work and didn't see why she should have to work and that she'd sooner break the place up. I reassured her that she wouldn't have to work here any longer, and at 9 am promptly rang the social worker and asked her to remove her, which she quickly did. What must she have been like *without* the drugs?

To add to the excitement of the morning, Anne came running to me at 8 am to tell me that the new guest, Mrs Cornish, who'd arrived the day before, had had an accident and was lying half under the bed with her nightdress half off. I called Jim and we gasped when we saw her.

She looked half dead, with one arm out of her nightdress and her head sticking out from under the bed.

The daughter had told us the previous day, "You will see that Mother has whisky when she wants it, won't you?"

We'd assured her that we would. That evening Mrs Cornish asked Jim if she could buy a bottle of whisky. He gave her a bottle.

"Your daughter can buy a bottle and replace it when she comes. Don't worry about the money," he said. She left the lounge at 9.30 pm and I saw her in bed at 10 pm, and said "goodnight".

Now here she was "out for the count" with the empty whisky bottle beside her. Since this little episode she gets a thimble full per night! If only the daughter had said she rationed the whisky, this incident could have been avoided. She's well now, but everything happens in triplicate. Have you noticed? During that morning we had a phone call from a guest's relatives who often came to dinner, telling us that they'd had a friend fly over from South Africa to visit them, and as they were coming that night to see us, could they bring him?

"Yes", I said, "we'll be delighted."

They arrived and we were introduced to a tall bearded man with a coat nearly down to his ankles, who spoke like Montgomery. Jim handed out drinks and asked him what he'd like.

"Don't drink! Don't drink!" he snapped.

"Oh dear, he's quite eccentric. This is going to be a lively evening," I thought. He agreed he'd have coffee, so I left them and returned with the coffee to find them discussing South Africa.

One of our friends said, "It was lovely in South Africa when I was nursing there 20 years ago, but I hear it has all changed now — tension everywhere."

The eccentric jumped to his feet.

"Trouble makers. Trouble makers. They're all trouble makers. Off with their blanks. Off with their blanks," He screamed. Jim jumped to his feet.

"I don't want their bloody blanks cut off. It's people like you that create tension instead of peace," he said. His face was red. I can't honestly say whose was redder as our friends said. "We'd better be on our way, and if it's all right with you we'll see you on Sunday."

They phoned and apologised when they got back, and the following Sunday discussed his behaviour while having dinner with us. They agreed he was shockingly rude, but was feted by most people because his father had been famous. I do love Jim, Tilly. He's idealistic and brave.

A few days after all this, Joe Harris, the local policeman, called in to ask us if we'd heard any suspicious noises, as our nearest neighbour had returned from London to find the house was only a shell. A furniture van had driven through the fields and stripped their home, a large five-bedroom house full of antiques. Naturally, we couldn't have heard anything. It's too far away from us.

This reminds me that that house and this one share the back drive, and the sewerage pipes from both houses run under the farmer's field. Several times the tractors have broken the sewerage pipes and, under the terms of the lease, Jim has to pay part of the cost to replace the pipes each time they're broken, which doesn't seem fair when we didn't break them. However, life's unfair for millions, so we always paid without a fuss. The back drive was beginning to develop large pot-holes and the neighbours approached us about getting them filled in and sharing the costs. By coincidence, a man had come touting for business to repair drives, so we agreed for him and his men to do the repairs.

They worked a few days and Jim gave them a cheque for £250 and got a receipt. This figure included the gravel and tar, etc. The neighbours saw the work completed and said they were going abroad. Six weeks later they came back and — horror of horrors — pot-holes had begun to show in the drive. They phoned up and I answered. They refused to pay their share of the bill!

We phoned Joe Harris the local constable. He came over and inspected the receipt and told us that the men had repaired other drives and vanished into the night leaving other irate householders to discover that they'd been done, as weeks later pot-holes appeared in their drives, too. I took the receipt to the neighbours and reminded them that we'd always paid for the broken pipes of the sewerage and that they had got out of paying their share, and that we had never broken our word. They settled up with us amicably and all was well.

Tilly, with all the unplanned events that take place you must think me mad at my age to like playing practical jokes. However, I don't play them very often, and I think I ought to pack up after what happened last week. When our friends came back to dinner after the incident over the eccentric guest, they discussed a houseboat that her sister and husband had just bought on the Thames after working abroad for 25 years. The subject of practical jokes arose, and it was agreed that we should play one on them; but what?

"I know. Tell them there are teredo worms in the river and that the river police are asking boat owners to take part in an experiment, by lowering a fresh loaf in a plastic bag into the river and drawing it up every day to see how many teredo worms have got through to the bait," said Jim. We worked on this idea, and I suggested that a tall handsome 18-year-old son of another friend could phone them.

Jim said, "Tell him to say he's Inspector Gregson," thinking of Sherlock Holmes.

The next morning I phoned our friends' son, Nick, and explained the idea. He phoned back within 15 minutes to say it had worked a treat as he had explained that they couldn't afford to use dozens of divers to check on the amount of teredo worms in the river, and that he would call and inspect the plastic bag and contents on Friday night, which of course he would not do.

Friday night arrived and our social worker friend had just arrived to spend a couple of hours with us. Jim poured her a drink and the phone rang. He answered and became very worried. He hung up.

"It has all gone wrong," he said. "Quick, phone Nick and tell him not to go near the boat."

"Don't be silly, he's not going to the boat. He agreed," I said.

"You must phone at once to be sure."

"Nonsense," I replied.

"Well, I'll phone," said Jim.

"How could you not believe me?" I said and rushed out of the room. He followed me and phoned the boat from the office, and told them that he'd engineered the joke and was sorry it had gone wrong. They were apparently relieved because I heard Jim joking with them and agreeing that we'd see them next week.

They had phoned the river police on Friday morning and asked to speak to Inspector Gregson and were told that he didn't exist, there wasn't any teredo worm, and that they ought to take precautions against anyone coming to their boat that night and claiming that they came from the river police. Their 17-year-old son who was at a public school had been informed, so he'd arrived on the boat with half a dozen young men ready to take the supposed Inspector Gregson to pieces.

Later, I phoned the sister and brother who'd heard from them how they'd lowered the bread in the plastic bag in the Thames daily, and were at this moment trying to work out something to play back on us!

By the time they think up a joke I'll be caught, because I'm sure they'll leave it for a while.

It's time for bed and we look forward to all your news.

Much love,
Lillian.

Tilly my love,

Another two days and we will be on the *Uganda*. We'll also be staying in Portugal for two weeks after visiting Morocco, Madeira and Lisbon, and so on. So I thought I would hastily write, as I'm sure there will be lots to write about when we get back.

First sit back while I tell you about Miss Capper, a bright 74-year-old, who could pass for 60. Miss Capper had been shown round the place and declared it to be exactly what she wanted and arrangements were made for her to move in in the following week. A few days later Jim had a phone call from a well-known aristocrat who informed him that Miss Capper was a relative, and that he would be keeping a close eye on the place to ensure that she hadn't any complaints, and if she had he would be taking action. Jim was furious and told him that she would have to prove that she was fit to mix with the other residents, and if she wasn't she would be given notice.

The first week she bustled here and there and up and down to the village, and seemed very efficient and capable. The second week she said she was going shopping and would like to take Jim's aunt and Mrs Raidell.

"They are a responsibility. They haven't any memories, so it would mean you would have to keep tight hold of their arms or they would get lost," Jim reminded her.

"No problem at all! You can rest assured they will be perfectly all right with me," she said.

Off they went, the three of them. Jim was worried by one o'clock and frantic by three o'clock. At 10 past three an even more frantic taxi driver turned up with them.

He said, "I told her to keep a tight hold of their arms. When I went back to collect her at noon she was wringing her hands, saying, 'Those silly women. They're stupid. I left them outside Woolworth's, and told them not to move until I got back'." He said he had been searching everywhere for them, and was just going to report to the police when he found them. That's the last time she takes anyone out, we thought.

A few weeks passed and then Rose handed me a magnificent mink coat.

"You take this. Miss Capper's gone round the bend," she said. "It arrived by post this morning and she said it was my present and would I post some letters for her, but look where they are addressed to!"

I read them. Harrods, Aspreys, Marshall and Snelgrove, Liberty's and Bourne and Hollingsworth.

"You're right Rose. We'll lock the coat in the office, and 'His Highness' can take it away when he collects her. Meanwhile I'll have a word with him."

I rang him.

"Ellen can do what she likes with her money. She's got the interest for life, but can't touch the capital," he said.

"This coat cost thousands and I am going to open these letters and look at the cheques, and check what she intends to buy," I retorted. The amounts varied from £200 to £800. He told me to post them.

"Certainly not," I protested. "She's got to be protected, and so have my staff. I don't want any investigations about my staff after she's dead," I informed him.

A week passed and there was a Red Cross sale in the village. We were all astonished when the taxi driver came in with pot plant after pot plant, jewellery, cakes, buns, flowers, books, jumpers and shawls. He made journey after journey up to Miss Capper's room which by now we could hardly get into.

She'd said to two of the stall-holders, "I've got a lot of friends and all the old people to buy things for. I want to pay for the lot." She got a taxi and brought it back.

Two days later "His Highness" came to collect her to go on holiday. Thank God Jim was out. She insisted that everything she bought went into "His Highness's" car. He was furious, his face became redder and redder each time he came down the stairs until he had filled the car!

Two weeks after this Miss Capper had been back a few days when we were wakened at 2 am by a terrible screaming outside the bedroom door. We rushed out and it was a sight to behold . There lay Miss Capper covered in faeces, screaming. I layered newspaper on the floor, then removed her clothes, and bathed her, and eventually put her to bed helped by Jim.

"I might scream again tomorrow!" she said.

Jim shook his head and said, "Not here, she won't."

I phoned the doctor who reported that she was a manic-depressive, at the moment had "verbal diarrhoea", and should go to a nursing home. We phoned "His Highness" and explained the situation. He arrived at 7 pm. After 10 minutes he burst into tears, said Ellen loved us, and begged us to keep her. We gave in, and I spoon-fed and washed her each day for two weeks. Then she had a bad haemorrhage and the doctor removed her to hospital. Later that week they phoned me and said she had recovered and could be brought back.

"No she can't. I'm coming in to see her," I said. We could see she was in a hopeless condition and hadn't recovered at all. She died the next day. A very sad tale.

The screaming of Miss Capper reminds me that we had to have poor

Miss Jane put into a nursing home. She rushed round hammering at the guests' bedroom doors at midnight shouting and screaming, "My mother and father are outside. Let them in!" We felt sorry. She had been with us for some years.

Fiona Hart stayed overnight and, when discussing Miss Capper and Miss Jane, she said, "Lillian, I don't know how you can do it. I couldn't touch anyone in that condition." I bit my tongue. *Everyone* can do it, especially those who have brought up children. I've often felt sick myself when cleaning someone up, but I feel so sorry for the person who's in such a condition because they can't do it for themselves. Anyway, if one was paid three times as much as an MP to do the job, there wouldn't be any shortage of people, and I suspect a few MPs would be wearing rubber gloves and overalls!

Jim dreamt that we'd retired after keeping a circus, but kept the pet lion named Wallace. I was sitting up in bed with a primus stove on my lap stirring tomato soup for Wallace's breakfast. Wallace was lying between us stretching and yawning. Jim got out of bed and said, "Here you, be careful. If you splash him with that he might eat us." We fell about laughing at this silly dream.

What isn't so silly is that I've got recorded, six weeks ago, twice in a week, that I dreamed the butcher was desperately searching everywhere for his children. Last week Rose told me that the villagers are upset. On Tuesday night he washed his three children; two, four and six years of age, played with them in front of the television and then put them to bed. At 9pm he was off on his one and only weekly night visit to the Buffs. Kissing his wife (she is 26, he is 40) he said, "Do you want me to bring you back a drink, chick?"

She smiled and said, "No".

When he returned, half of the household equipment, the children and the new car he had bought her, had disappeared. She'd run off with a 20-year-old dropout.

Well, Tilly, the sun is shining and I've got lots to do, so I'll away and get started. Pity I've got two extra ribs. Because of these I go through hell for the first five minutes in the morning. Jim calls me his little brontosaurus! Take care of yourself. Will send you plenty of cards.

Much love,
Lillian.

My dear Tilly,

Thank you for the phone calls and letter. Before I tell you about the holiday let me fill you in with the story of Isla. I dashed up to London to a hostel which had been recommended to me as the perfect place to find a suitable person to help us, and I was introduced to a New Zealand doctor's wife. She was pretty, vivacious, and an extremely efficient type of personality, or so one thought. She said she was divorced and had come to England to see her daughter. She'd collapsed on the street, had been taken to hospital, and removed here. I arranged for her to come to tea and be interviewed on Sunday.

We thought we'd had a miracle happen the way she spoke. She could cook, nurse, etc, etc. We needn't worry, she'd help the matron and all the staff. So Isla moved in!

On the Tuesday I had prepared fairy cakes for afternoon tea and, when they were cooked, I put two fruit cakes covered with butter papers in the gas oven, and left Isla in the kitchen, with Jenny to supervise, while I went out. Passing the kitchen on my way out I smelt burnt paper. I checked the kitchen. Isla had removed the butter papers and put newspapers over the cakes. Newspapers in a gas oven!! I got her daughter's number from her, and phoned. She said it was unfortunate, but her mother was as nutty as a fruit cake. The father, who was a doctor, had had to divorce her and the youngest brother had tried to commit suicide over her. She had attempted to look after her mother, but discovered they couldn't leave her in the house. She was too dangerous. I decided to have a word with Isla.

"You can stay in your room and go for walks," I said, "but you can come into the building only at mealtimes. I don't want to put you on the street. I'll help you find a job when I come back from my holiday." I told her I hoped to find her a post where there was a large staff where someone could keep an eye on her.

We warned Mrs Neal when she arrived to take over, and hoped things would work out all right. It did while we were away and then I set to and got her a job as a companion where there were other staff. Within three weeks the old lady had fallen and broken a femur and we had an ecstatic letter from Isla telling us that she had met a handsome, wealthy ecclesiastic at the old lady's, and he had proposed marriage and she was going on a tour of Europe with him. She sent cards from different parts of Europe, followed by a letter on her return, to say the marriage was off because he had got something wrong with his little willie! I wonder what? I reckon it atrophied in despair at some of Isla's antics.

We were glad to see them all when we returned and they all greeted us with delight. Peter the Pug sang! Silvy wouldn't leave me. It was gorgeous to see all the happy faces. Mrs Neal was liked by all, but the staff said they fell about laughing. Every afternoon she practised cake making to no avail. Nobody ate them. There had been a confrontation on the day after we left. She had ordered Rose to change six sheets because she found tea stains on them, and Rose refused, quite rightly, telling her that she had been in charge of linen for 10 years, and if she was to change for a tea stain, sheets would have to be changed every day.

"They're changed once a week unless anyone is ill and then they're changed whenever necessary," said Rose.

We thanked Mrs Neal for being so kind, and arranged that she would take charge on our next holiday if she was free. I asked her how she had enjoyed it compared to being a hospital matron.

"Much better, but I have had a working partnership in a nursing home," she informed us.

"What happened?" we asked.

"Oh, he went bankrupt. He blamed me, but as I told him, that was nonsense. If you spend twopence here you make fourpence there." Ah, there's the rub, Tilly dear. As you know better than me, that is not the way a business runs, or at least not for long.

Now for the holiday. Jim had phoned the travel agent's office to check if we needed inoculations.

"Not necessary," said the official.

We unpacked our luggage on the *Uganda* and then heard a message over the tannoy system asking us both to report to the doctor. A mistake had been made. We hadn't been asked if we intended to go ashore in a foreign country and if we were then we must be inoculated! The inoculations over, we relaxed. It was lovely to do so. While we were in Morocco the heat was stifling, and my head felt as though it was going to burst with the hammering inside it. Guides took us through very narrow streets packed with animals and people. It was very colourful, but also one noticed the dirt and poverty. Eventually we were taken to a Moorish restaurant where we all sat on cushions round a round table. A giant copper bowl full of a steaming tomato concoction was set in the centre of the table, and some of the tourists said they wouldn't eat without a knife and fork.

The waiter said, "Now you are in our country, you must adapt yourself to our customs". They protested.

"No, this is fun," I said, and, picking up a piece of bread, began dipping it in the mixture.

Fifteen minutes later they removed the copper dish still nearly two thirds full and Jim said, "I expect that will be topped up for the next lot."

An enormous pile of semolina with lamb chops placed around it was the next course, and finally a large dish of fresh, washed fruit. My head thumped away. I dreaded the journey back through the desert and when they finally washed our hands with rosewater I was pleased to leave and climb in the coach. I can hardly remember the journey back. Jim called the doctor when we got on board. He sympathised, said it was the inoculations that had caused it, and put me out instantly with an injection.

Madeira! Ah! that was exciting. Beautiful, but no beach to write home about. We went up by coach to the steepest cliff face in the world. The coach didn't go right to the top. We left it and walked the last five minutes of the journey. We took photographs, admired the scenery and were the last to stroll back to the bus.

As we passed a taxi crammed with tourists going to the top, we saw lying in the hedge, a man without any legs, and no hope of dole or sickness benefit.

Let's see if we can find some Escudos for him, Jim," I said.

Horrors, I'd left my bag with passports and money on the top while I took photographs. I was sure it must be gone by now, and we raced like mad uphill and arrived completely out of breath to find everyone too busy to notice the big white handbag in their midst. God paid me back that minute. Our holiday would have been ruined without passports or money.

The next day we went up over 4,000 feet and came back down the last thousand feet by toboggan. We were told it was the law that every child was educated, but we couldn't see how the hundreds of families working on the steep terraces could get their children down to school every day.

The next stop was Lisbon, where we left the ship, having arranged to pick it up there a fortnight later on the next round trip. We went to Estoril where we had booked in for three days before continuing to spend 10 days in the Algarve. The hotel in Estoril was set in the most delightful colourful garden you can imagine, and the owner's equally colourful pet parrot had the freedom of the garden. It was enchanting there, but at the beginning all was chaos.

We announced our names to two Portuguese maids who waved wildly and, speaking rapidly in Portuguese, waved us away. A gentleman rose from his seat in the garden and acted as interpreter. He said the hotel was full up and we'd made a mistake. We produced evidence of the booking, and the maids went inside shrugging shoulders, vociferously gabbling about the stupidity of Madame, according to our interpreter. They came back with a tray of coffee and it was explained that Madame would arrange something if we had patience!

Nearly an hour later the most stunning looking Madame, about 30 years of age, descended the steps into the garden. She apologised overwhelmingly, telling us that she was always overbooking. Her English parents had died and left her the house, and she had come back five years ago to run it as a hotel. She had rung another hotel who would accommodate us for one night, and the maids would take our luggage and bring it back the next day. So we followed the two hefty maids up the narrow street, each one carrying our heavy cases on her shoulders!

The hotel! It was ghastly! The beds I'd like to forget about as they had the lumpiest mattresses you could imagine. The food was tasteless watery soup, the meat as tough as blazes, and we couldn't recognise what animal it came from. We only slept fitfully and were pleased to see the dawn.

At 10 am the maids arrived with the luggage back at the hotel we had booked into, and we decided to spend the day in Lisbon. Tilly, the churches were magnificent. Incredible, unbelievable craftsmanship, yet as I gazed in awe I remembered the cruelty and loss of lives caused by the search for gold and treasures. I thought, if only these treasures had been obtained through love and not violence.

We arrived back at 6 pm and later sat down to a dinner that would have caused a normal Englishman to enquire of his wife if she wanted a divorce. We spent the rest of the evening sitting in the garden and were joined at 10 pm by an English couple with two teenage children. They described their evening, and they were annoyed because they had seen a dirty run-down little cafe and thought, we'll eat in here it will be cheap. They had a small plate of scampi only and were presented with a bill for £8. They calmed down over a drink and we laughed and talked until midnight.

The next day the police brought an Englishman to the hotel. He had arrived from Peru the day before, booked into the hotel, gone out on the town, got drunk and forgot the name of the hotel! He was a diplomat, the owner told us, and always stayed there when he was in Portugal. He always got drunk and forgot who he was and what the hotel was called!

The next day we also spent in Lisbon. The embroidery, lacework, and silver were superb. We finished off the day talking with other guests about the sights we had all seen, and went to bed hoping that the food situation would improve in the Algarve.

At 3 pm the next day we arrived at Portimao collecting the car we had hired at the garage. We discovered the owners had worked in England some years ago and had a good command of the language.

82

Two hefty maids carried our heavy cases
on their shoulders.

Commander and Mrs Dobbs, the English Naval Officer and wife we were going to stay with, had sent instructions on how to get from Portimao to Rasmalho, but the garage owners insisted that we must cross the bridge which wasn't mentioned by Commander Dobbs. It was boiling hot — Jim had to hold the wheel with handkerchiefs and and we drove endlessly on and on.

Fifteen minutes later Jim said, "There's something wrong. I know it. They misdirected us at that garage".

The sun shone from the deepest blue sky I've ever seen. We were both sticky and uncomfortable when we arrived in the centre of a square. Every building was pure white, and not a soul was in sight. We thought they were probably all asleep as one couldn't work in this heat. Jim spotted a Post Office, and had the good fortune to find that the owner spoke French, as we could not speak Portuguese nor he English. He redirected us and we eventually arrived at the beautiful house of Commander Dobbs. They said they had been very worried and wondered where we'd got to. Later, they gave us an excellent meal, except for the meat. We were told that the meat situation was quite different there compared with England.

Commander Dobbs had come into the Navy through the war, unlike Jim who had been to Dartmouth. He was a good straight character and was living in the Algarve because he'd married the daughter of a rich woman who didn't approve of the marriage. They now had grown-up children in various places around the world. While living in England, Mummy used to visit them often, and had upset Michael Dobbs's apple cart. Mummy visited once *too* often and there was a blazing row, and he persuaded Daphne to sell their house and go out to the Algarve. Mummy had visited them out there once, and experienced a slight earthquake in which hundreds of rats had torn through the house, and she'd said she'd never come back again.

We listened with fascination to the stories about the different English people who lived there. It was like reading a Somerset Maugham novel. Daphne's eyes had been getting brighter and brighter, and every time she got up to get a drink her gait grew more unsteady. It was 11.30 pm when she suddenly lunged across the room, stood over me swaying wildly and said, "How dare you take a bloody holiday! Why didn't you stay in the country and make sure that horrible creature Harold Wilson was thrown out."

I was speechless. So was Jim.

Michael said sharply, "Daphne, Daphne, I've told you before not to bring up politics in front of visitors. That was unforgivable." But Daphne collapsed in her chair, venom in her eyes, muttering, "It's not right, that man wants chucking out."

Jim said, "We've had a tiring day. It's bedtime," and we bid them goodnight.

Every day we spent on the sands. They were so hot you couldn't walk on them without sandals, but the shock was the sea temperature. It was the coldest I've ever known and I've often gone swimming in the sea in November in England. They prepared a wonderful picnic lunch each day for us, and we'd have a drink with them in the bars between 10 am and 11 am, when they would introduce us to all the English inhabitants, We'd return at 6 pm, shower, and spend the rest of the evening after dinner exchanging tales and views — thank God without politics.

One funny story you should hear. When they first arrived they had to send their passports to Lisbon. It is the law of Portugal. Six weeks later they received a card to tell them their passports were in the Post Office at Portimao. When they showed the card to collect it they were refused.

"You must show your passport before you can collect letters," they were told. The argument grew louder and louder. Fifteen minutes later an angry Daphne stamped her foot and yelled, "You are stupido, stupido," and rushed across the road to order a drink at the table outside a café. The Postmaster rushed over and stood over her yelling in Portuguese. She started shouting again, "You are stupido."

Another customer intervened, and asked her what the problem was. He managed to calm them both down by explaining to the postmaster she was saying he was stupid and to Daphne that she had insulted him publicly in the worst possible way by calling him a homosexual! They got fined for not being in possession of their passports and then fined again for being fined. The lawyer pointed to the stone work round the court where it was chiselled that one must pay a fine for being fined!

One day we met a retired couple from Yorkshire. They rushed up to us as we were getting in the car.

"Are you residents or holidaymakers?", they asked.

"Holiday-makers," we informed them.

"My God, don't be tempted to become residents, we're still trying to get our passports back. I wrote and told them that their department employed a lot of Rip van Winkles. Now all I get are letters telling me that they are investigating my complaints about Rip van Winkles. We've been stuck here 18 months." We commiserated with them, wished them luck, and related the story later in the evening.

"He worked in a factory all his life and said he thought a hot country would help in getting rid of the rheumatism," Jim told Michael.

The next day Daphne and Michael said they would accompany us to Lisbon and have tea with us in their hotel before we caught the boat. They were to leave early, drive the car to a station an hour's drive away, where they would pick it up on the way back. I could not touch the melon on the last night. It was packed with fruit and cream and I didn't want to offend Daphne so I wrapped it in paper handkerchiefs and cardboard, and put it in my case to dispose of the next day. We'd been on the train half-an-hour when I panicked and thought I'd left the melon back in the bedroom. I hastily searched the cases, and, joy, found it and got rid of it.

Michael and Daphne met us at the station and took us to their hotel in the centre of Lisbon. The lift was so small that Michael and I went up first. Michael walked along the landing and announced in Portuguese to a dark-haired middle aged woman that we'd arrived. She went mad. She pushed him away from her and indicated that I was to be removed at once. I could see he was trying to explain something, but she just shook her head and, walking towards me, waved me to get out of the place speaking rapidly all the time.

The lift door opened, and out stepped Jim and Daphne who greeted Madame with a smile. Five minutes later tea was served in their room and Madame was happy. She knew Michael and Daphne well, and wasn't going to have any funny business in her hotel. She'd told him that he should be ashamed of himself with a nice wife like he had, thinking he could get away with bringing this terrible creature to her hotel!

Aboard the ship that night we talked of the toil-worn local inhabitants we'd seen in the Algarve, and of how they were probably half the age they looked. The summer sun probably accounts for much of the ageing of the skin.

We recalled Daphne's story of buying the washing machine for her maid, Maria, who brought all the villagers up to see it working. Two days later the wonder had worn off and it was never used again. All clothes were taken down to the river to be washed where one could enjoy exchanging one's problems and putting the world to rights with ones friends. Happy Maria.

Gosh, this has been a long letter. Will phone you next week and hope we get another holiday next year.

Much love,
Lillian.

6th JANUARY, 1969

My dear Tilly,

We were delighted to hear that you all enjoyed Christmas. Your letter was a tonic. When I phoned I told you that we had company, so I dare not spend a long time telling you the events that occurred here.

The Christmas party, a few days before Christmas, went off with a swing and also the carol singers and the Brownies, but I'm afraid we missed the big New Year's Eve party. At least I gave a drink to all the guests who were still on their feet.

It all began on Christmas Day. I began at 6 am. Everything was ready by noon, the tables laid with crackers, glasses, Christmas decorations etc. It looked fine. Thirteen guests sat down to dinner. Jim served the wines, I carved the turkey, Anne served the lunches, Mai and Doreen brought the vegetables to the table. I'd taken six plates in with me from the bottom of the Rayburn and asked Mai to warm the rest. I didn't know what it was, but the staff seemed miles away, and when I'd served the first six, I sent Anne for the rest of the plates. I turned to take them quickly out of her hands and they were boiling hot! They'd been put in the top of the Rayburn. I yelled as they crashed on the floor, ran into the hall and had a good cry! Jim came after me and comforted me. I returned and tried to make the guests laugh.

Once the washing up was done we returned to the dining room with the staff and all sat down. All faces were long, and the dinner was only picked at and also the pudding. We pulled crackers, but it was flat and dismal, so once the staff had gone off duty I took Jim's temperature — 103°! I took the temperatures of the rest of the staff and they registered between a 101° and 103°. I had to put them all to bed. There were chickens and geese to be attended to, hot water bottles to be filled, and the evening meal to be dealt with all by myself!

I got up at 5 am the next morning to get the vegetables prepared and poultry fed before I began the breakfasts. There would be no outside staff for four days, so I raced round with breakfasts, hot or cold drinks for the patients, collected the trays, washed up, and prepared the lunch. I asked the guests to bear with me if meals were late, and they were wonderful. Blind Mrs Hart insisted on helping to dry up with another four guests who also insisted on helping. At first I said I could cope, but I was soon glad of the help as I noticed other guests showing symptons of 'flu. Within 48 hours I had 14 in bed. To add to the problems, six had diarrhoea and that meant the copper going all the afternoon as I boiled and spun dry the washed linen.

Jim kept asking me why I spent so much time gossiping instead of sitting with him, but I wasn't going to let him know what had happened, as his temperature was still bordering on a hundred. On Monday the 29th I was pleased to see Rose and Jenny back, but there was still too much to do. Mrs Hart's daughter, Fiona arrived at 11.30 am and after hearing the saga from her mother, said, "I must see poor Jim." She entered the bedroom with a glass of gin in her hand and shrieked, "Jim, darling, how awfully beastly for you. Mummy told me how awfully hard Lillian has had to work, with three staff, and 14 guests in bed."

I wish she hadn't as he insisted on getting up, and at 6 pm on Wednesday night I had to call the doctor out. He'd collapsed with bronchial pneumonia. By this time, thank God, all except two guests and two staff were back to normal, but it was an ominous start to the year. Jim recovered 10 days later.

Within two months we had seven vacancies. Three guests had died of strokes, the padre died in hospital, as did Mr Hope and Mr Terry, as the aftermath of operations, and Miss Wallace injured her foot, but the massive doses of antibiotics failed to save her. She had developed gangrene. I nursed her until the end.

Jim got better and we looked at the accounts. Now I was free from the worry of nursing, I realised I'd been silly in not cancelling part of the milk. We were taking £17,000, our expenses were over £15,000 and, taking into consideration Jim's pension, we paid £1,000 in tax! Now we were down to £12,000. I cut the milk by a third temporarily, and then we got on with decorating the vacant bedrooms where necessary.

By the middle of April we were full up again. The outstanding memory I had of all this was listening to the ambulance men standing in the hall as Rose packed Mr Terry's case ready to go to hospital. They stared round unaware of me standing out of sight on the landing.

"It's all right for some. Look at this place. Look at the money here."

Second ambulance man, "Yes, too bloody true mate. I bet the owners are drunk half the time, or spending the lolly for months in some Caribbean island. You don't wonder that the working man gets fed up. And look what happens when someone's ill. They don't want to know. Stick them in the hospital. What's wanted is a bloody revolution in the country, and these places handed over to the local authority."

I ran down the back stairs and, moving into the hall, invited them to come up to Mr Terry's room. They were most courteous to me.

The first driver said, "This is a big place. Many people work here?"

"There are six staff," I replied.

"I should have thought you needed 16 at least in a place this size. Do they treat you well?"

"Excellently."

With that we reached Mr Terry's room and I escorted him into the ambulance and asked them to wait while I collected my coat. I was back within the hour and hastily wrote down the conversation in my diary and thought that the more knowledge we gain the more we understand how very little we know.

If everything goes well we'll try and arrange to go on holiday this year. We could both do with one. I've spoken to the doctor, and he's going to contact a matron who is a friend and see if she will take over for a month. I've started to prepare some menus and thought about employing extra help, so we have something exciting to look forward to.

We have taken on two new members of the staff, one from the same psychiatric hospital as the others came from, and one from the hospital for the subnormal. The first is a young girl of 23 who apparently falls easily in love, spends what money she earns on a boy, and then attempts suicide when he drops her. She's just got over her fifth attempt. The second, named Katy, came through the arrangement of a new guest's brother who is a doctor at the subnormal hospital. He warned me that she'd had a lot of babies plus VD. Several of the babies had been a result of the relationships she'd formed with patients in the hospital who were also subnormal, and that it was an offence for a man knowingly to have sex with a subnormal girl, so I would have to take extra precautions to see she didn't get pregnant again. I said I would arrange her days off with Anne, but I won't be able to arrange her holiday until next year. I've just arranged for Anne to realise her life's dream. I'm taking her to London and putting her in the hands of a Catholic party going to Lourdes on a pilgrimage.

They are both pleasant and do their jobs to our satisfaction. Katy seems to love it here. She is 37, plump but attractive, with gorgeous auburn hair. We'll keep our fingers crossed that all goes well.

The new guests are interesting. Miss Mainwaring is a rich, capable 90-year-old and Miss Judd a spritely, smart 70-year-old. Dr Keynes, a handsome batchelor of 88, and very "with it", and Mrs Haines, an 82-year-old tall, elegant lady with a beautiful and pleasing accent.

Mrs Haines's story is very sad. Fifty years before she had stepped into the hall of her house, and her husband, who was ill and had two nurses in attendance, staggered out of bed, while they were out of the room, on to the landing. He leaned over the bannister and crashed to death on his head on the marble floor. From that moment she had been confined in a private psychiatric hospital which closed down six weeks ago. She had always been allowed to use oil lamps there because she had a hatred of electricity and somehow associated her husband's death with it.

We agreed to let her use oil lamps, but a week later I found one smashed on the floor, so I rethought it out. We bought two massive imitation oil lamps that had electric bulbs and arranged for her daughter to take her out for the day. The electricians fixed them to the ceiling in her bedroom and bathroom and then blanked the switch so that she couldn't switch them on or off, but would have a permanently low light.

When she returned we said, "Look what God has done for you! He has arranged for you to have your own permanent oil supply." She quickly switched the light on and off, and finding it hadn't any effect she accepted it, thank God.

She asked me not to let anyone come to the room on Sunday mornings as she said she holds a service for all God's Angels and they come through the walls and the room is filled with a golden light. I've just remembered that's supposed to be the haunted room in the house. The Vet said he visited here 30 years ago and his dogs and the owners dogs would not go near that room and backed away, snarling, from the door.

Well, Tilly, I'll phone as usual next week. Look forward to your letter.

Much love,
Lillian.

My dear Tilly,

Glad to hear your voice the other night and to know that all is well. I agree with you that it would be better to sell your house and move. When the farmer removed the trees and hedges, because you won the case over the right to keep the road free from cars parking, I never thought that terrible rain-floods would result. What a shame you have to use gumboots for weeks after heavy rain. In any case, you won't want to be so cut off as you're getting older. I'll ring next week. Here's the promised news.

Mrs Neal said she would only be free during the month of April, so we booked a three week trip to 10 countries, starting by flying to Venice on April 3 to board the SS *Misteria*. We'd arranged to stay in London for two days with a charming friend named Alison who is a lecturer. When we arrived she looked awful. The poor soul had got 'flu.

"I rang early to prevent you coming, in case you got the 'flu and spoilt your holiday," she told us.

"Don't worry about us. What can we do for you?" we asked. And so we stayed the two days, taking her teenage twins out to lunch each day.

The following day after flying to Venice, we boarded the SS *Misteria* together with more than 500 tourists of every nationality.

We were allocated a good cabin, fortunately, because there were only about half a dozen cabins that one couldn't criticize on the ship. Other passengers complained to us later of overcrowding and overheating. Anyway, we made our way to the dining room after unpacking. It was chaotic in there, but we were eventually seated opposite a little old Welsh lady and an attractive Australian widow who appeared to be in her 30s. We introduced ourselves, and Jim ordered champagne and invited them to join us telling them it was my birthday on April 3.

After one glass of champagne the old lady said she felt ill but hadn't got a cabin to go to. I offered to sort it out and took the old lady to the purser's office. She argued and argued that she would not accept the cabin they had put her luggage in, as she said her brother had paid for a single cabin and she wasn't going to share. Three quarters of an hour later, after I'd persuaded her to accept, and saw her safely tucked up, I returned to find a very inebriated widow. She suddenly began to give us her opinion of the British people.

"You know what you are. You're God-dam Pommie bastards." She continued, "You're a bunch of God-dam idlers; you don't want to work, you're work-shy. You live for handouts and where do the bloody handouts come from? A handful of people who work. The rest of you God-dam idlers live off their backs. You wanna know something? Out in Australia people work. That's why you God-dam Pommies come rushing back from there, because you don't like work."

I got up and went back to the cabin. Jim followed me. I was reduced to tears. If the ship hadn't left port by now, I think I would have got off.

"I can't face three weeks of her," I cried. Jim agreed. We fell asleep and woke refreshed. In the dining room an officer apologised for the mix-up the previous night and introduced us to a Commander Bakewell and his daughter June, with whom we shared the table for the rest of the voyage, except for that night and the last night, when we joined the captain's table. The last night without Commander Bakewell and June was due to unexpected events which I'll soon come to.

We docked in Alexandria. I rushed on deck to take photographs and found the camera snatched out of my hand by Jim, as he'd spotted the notices I hadn't, all around the docks, indicating that anyone taking photographs would be arrested. We boarded a coach for Cairo, and when we arrived at the hotel made straight for the bathroom to cool off. In the bar they asked for about £2 each for gin and tonic and orange juice, and we refused them although we were gasping. I looked at Jim's eyes and spotted that they were filled with discharge. I'd remembered to bring a thermometer with me. Yes, he'd got a temperature of over 102°. He'd got 'flu. He refused to go to bed and we went down to dinner, where again they asked for £4 for drinks. Again we refused. Eventually the waiter said we could have them for £2, and we accepted.

The next day, on the way back to the ship, we stopped at an hotel and I asked for water, after having an orange juice which had been paid for together with the meal. They refused me as I hadn't any money left. Tilly, I was astounded. I know that water is precious in the desert, but they'd been well paid for the meals. I don't doubt the problem was that we'd got separated from our new friends, David and June, so I had to wait until we got back to the boat!

David had brought June on the voyage as a treat to help her get over an unhappy love affair. She was 21 years of age. We also made friends with a charming 40-year-old Welsh widow and her 18-year-old son, and wondered if David and Jean (the Welsh widow) might fall in love. Jim thought the good looking young boy was showing a lot of interest in June and that's where love would flourish.

"No, she's besotted by the handsome 40-year-old Greek captain. She never takes her eyes off him," I said.

92

The next day we left for Israel and, the first morning after we arrived there, we found all the coaches lined up to take us to Jerusalem. I refused to go because Jim still had a temperature, but he insisted as he'd been there before. I sat beside a pleasant, happy, brave, 40-year-old woman, who only had four months at the most to live. She said she had only one regret and that was that she wouldn't live to see her small daughter — whom she and her husband had brought on the voyage — married. The entire company of the ship knew and were wonderful to her.

In Jerusalem I felt both wonder and disgust — disgust at the commercialisation. As the Arabs tried to tempt us into the shops in the Souk to buy religious souvenirs, so the couriers hurried us along, telling us that we must buy from the new shop, a vast modern glass emporium.

"But we can't cash cheques," I protested.

"Oh yes, you can all cash cheques. You are standing on British soil in Jordan now!" he said. I wonder how many believed it! I bought rosaries for the staff and then had lunch before returning to the ship.

The following day Jim felt better and decided to come with us to Nazareth and Galilee. In Nazareth an Arab boarded the bus and tried to sell me a chain of wooden camels for a pound, exactly the same as I'd bought a few days before in Egypt for five shillings. I remarked on this.

"You pay this man. He's got two wives to keep," said the courier. I refused to buy, but I noticed that after he'd sold nearly everything in his basket, he shared the money with the courier. Ah, perhaps the courier has two wives also!

The magic part of the trip was Galilee, completely unspoilt. One felt humble yet inspired. It was the most deeply felt religious experience of one's life, just standing there.

We got back to the ship and, late that night, we were all still discussing the events and conversations of the day.

"They may be at war, but you can see in some cases they are brothers under the skin, especially when it comes to money, and as again with North and South Welsh, or the Chinese you have completely different outlooks among the same nationalities and good and bad in each one," we concluded.

Athens wasn't unfamiliar to either of us. I had been there soon after 1945 and, in any case, I had a friend there who owed me a hundred pounds which I was able to collect. It helped us to go ashore in the other countries, because we are not the type to smuggle money out of the country. But I'll tell you something — about three quarters of the British passengers did! One boasted in front of us that it was easy and opened a box of paper handkerchiefs that he'd resealed, stuffed with

£5 notes. The man was a fool. Fancy risking ruining your character to buy some worthless trinkets!

For as many British people that would break the law of their country, so as many of other nationalities would break the laws of their countries for money, which is truly the root of all evil. Money and power corrupt absolutely. Part of the corruption of power is the desire to tell other people what to do, instead of wanting to do for other people, which is the joy of Christ.

I'm not writing about the places we visited in chronological order, only as fast as my thoughts come. We visited Olympia where the wisteria, lilac, oranges and lemons were beautiful, as also was the marble statue of Hermes sculptured by Praxiteles about 900 BC. Zeus and Apollo were gigantic, but not as good. I forgot — back in Athens an American boy of about eight years of age, on viewing the scaffolding at the Acropolis where they were doing repair work said, "Haven't they finished it yet?".

We disembarked at Gruda and drove to Dubrovnik after a tour through the Amlla valley. We stood looking at the one and only bronze figure of Michael Spaggoti. The guide said that they didn't believe in the cult of personality. Jim pointed to a car within the city wall and told her we'd been informed that they weren't allowed.

"The regime allows a car as a privilege and, by using our imagination, we can all share the party leader's privilege", she replied. She was half smiling. Jim was aghast at the changes in Dubrovnik from when he'd last seen it as a young boy in 1934, when shops were overflowing with every type of merchandise and craftsmanship. Today the city feels as though it has come to a standstill. The few shops sell carved pieces of wood, or a few bits of rough, badly worked silver jewellery. We didn't see anything else; certainly no clothes, gold, paintings or lace, etc.

The snowcapped mountains and five million olive trees at Delphi will always be remembered, and also the frescos at Knossos, and the deep blue sea at Corfu, Limassol and Delos.

I woke up at Rhodes feeling really ill. I'd got 'flu, but didn't tell Jim because he would have refused to go ashore without me, and it was the only place he hadn't visited before. So I staggered up and down the street of the Knights beside him, peering through watery eyes at beautiful mosaic and marble floors in the Temple of Apollo, the Stadium of Diogones and the Mosque of Sulieman the Magnificent. We then drove on to Lindos where we admired the beautiful bay and returned to the ship with the idea of going to bed once we'd had something to drink. A harassed David met us.

"We didn't come with you today because I thought June was having a sleep when she didn't answer my knock. There's something wrong. She's still not awake. Will you come and look at her?" he asked. We went to her cabin where I took her pulse and examined her.

"She has taken an overdose. Get the doctor," I said to David. Jim went with him and returned to tell me that David couldn't speak Greek and couldn't make the doctor understand, so I went and asked him to hurry, in Greek. He was a very fat doctor with braces hanging to the floor down his back, and was looking under his bunk bed for his stethoscope. We arrived back in the cabin. He confirmed that she'd taken an overdose.

"Où est le flagon?" he asked in French.

"Here's the bottle. It's empty," I replied as I handed it to him.

"Clinic! Clinic!" he shouted, but in French it sounded like "cleeneek, cleeneek". He insisted I came with them, and all the way to the 'cleeneek' he kept tapping me on the shoulder and repeating, "Où est le flagon?" and ignored my answers. I'm glad it wasn't one of us that was ill! The young hospital doctor said June must stay there and, when she was moved into a ward, several Greek women stood in the doorway, and I overheard them describing the beautiful face of June.

I told David I'd pack her clothes for him, and that we would give him our Greek drachmas, which he could return later in England. I couldn't understand every word the Greek women were saying now, but it was enough to understand that they thought I was responsible for the suicide. They had gathered I wasn't the mother, and got some muddled story. As we left the clinic a ship's officer rushed in and said June must be brought back.

"If you take her back she'll do it again," I said.

"Why?"

"Because she thinks she is in love with your captain."

"No, no. She stays".

So the three of us went back to the ship. We said 'goodbye' to David and had a letter and the money returned last week. His daughter is better now.

As a result of all this, instead of sleeping in Venice one night we were able to have David's two seats on the plane when we arrived back in Venice.

We wandered round the shops for half an hour. Jim said, "You haven't bought anything for yourself," and bought me a lovely lace stole and garnet ring. We heard a recorded description of the golden screen in St Mark's Cathedral while viewing it. It had over 2,500 precious and semi-precious stones. We had a coffee — ten shillings each — in St Mark's Square, and took the water bus from St Brazzilio. For three hours we wandered, lost in the Doges' Palace. In the end Jim dragged me reluctantly down stone cellar steps and after a few minutes we heard American voices. It turned out to be the one day of the year all the guides at the Doges' Palace were on holiday! We just got to the airport in time to catch the plane.

Arriving back at midnight, we found a strange caravan in the grounds, which Mrs Neal said she knew nothing about, so we phoned Joe Harris, our local policeman. He woke the people up and I was sorry for them. It was Mr Shalk's son. He told us he was going to tell Mrs Neal that he would like to park there for the night, but his father had insisted he would tell her, and forgot!

Well Tilly dear, the most memorable moments that I will often relive are Galilee; the peasants farming in Egypt with the double-yoked oxen and plough; oxen turning slowly in a circle to pump the water; women carrying pots and buckets on their heads upright and proud; women washing clothes in the river. I felt as though I was back 2,000 years in time. The Pyramids I'll never forget, especially as the two camel drivers threatened to race my camel if I didn't give them back-sheesh. I only had a five pound note, so I sweated all the way, as I had said I would give them something when we got to the Pyramids.

"No, camel Captain see. He take from us. You give now, or camel gallop." It was pure blackmail, but I didn't give in though I was damned frightened.

God has been good to me to let me have such wonderful experiences. I don't deserve them, but I'll try and help others in return for the blessings I've had. The most forgettable sight was a toilet at an oasis an hour's drive from Cario. Ugh! I won't describe it. It would make you feel ill.

We really celebrated our anniversary yesterday, as we've spent days telling them about the holidays and listening to all the events that occurred here. Everything went well here, so we're happy all round. Two guests were taken ill. Miss Neal had them moved to hospital and I've brought them back.

Oh, a couple of days ago, one of the neighbours came into the kitchen and asked Jenny and Rose if the village baker sold stale cakes as she's giving a party for the old people from London! They were disgusted, but not as much as I was. She phoned and asked me to come and have coffee with her, as she had something she wanted to discuss with me, I went over. I nearly brought the coffee back when she came round saying what she wanted.

"I'm throwing a garden party for old people from London, and it's not very suitable to let them all come into the house to use the toilet. You've got a much bigger house and you're used to old people. Could they use yours?"

"You've got a downstairs toilet, and four bathrooms and toilets upstairs. I'm sure you'll manage very well. We wouldn't think it would be a good idea at all," I said. If she'd said "Do you mind if all our toilets are in use, and we have anyone desperate, can we send them over to you?" I would have said, "certainly". Well, this is the end of the trip, Tilly.

I'll phone you in a couple of days.

Much love,
Lillian.

1st JUNE, 1969

Dear Tilly,

We'll never be rich. I'm flaming. We've just returned from a session with the tax man. You remember the trip to the Algarve? Well, Jim paid a thousand pounds tax the week before we left. When he came back he found a demand for another thousand. He phoned our accountant who told him, "It's all right. Pay it, you'll get it back."

"But it doesn't make sense. We only made two thousand profit for the year," said Jim.

"They often do this. It will be put right, don't worry."

So Jim paid it. We've been fighting it for a year now. The head tax man said, "You shouldn't have had to pay it, but there's nothing you can do to get it back. It's not our fault. Your accountant only sent one letter when you first became a partnership. He didn't send the second letter confirming it."

"You mean we must claim it off him?" I said.

"That's your business not ours," said the tax man.

"But we've worked a year for nothing."

"I can't help that," he said.

We've phoned the accountant and he admits that if we go to law he'll lose his job with the firm, and he's got two children. Well, I don't want anyone to lose his job, so we've come to an agreement that instead of us paying him, he'll pay himself until he's worked it off! The reason they take so much tax is because Jim has a pension. They take our personal allowance out of that, so we don't get it on the business. Ah well, Tilly, that's life, but it makes you mad when you know that you save the country money by working.

Rose told me today that the man who lives opposite has four children, hasn't worked in 15 years, drives a car, and is at the pub most nights. What makes Rose so wild, she said, is that because they save for a holiday once a year, they have never been able to afford a car, and her husband's only drink is a couple of pints on a Saturday night. I feel like Robin Hood, that I would be perfectly justified in taking half that tax man's salary for the year, and giving it to the poor. I'm so annoyed!

I wonder what Jack Jones or any of the Union heads would say if the tax man took, say two thousand, off them, instead of a thousand! You can be sure these figures are peanuts as far as they're concerned.

I must forget it now and tell you what else has happened. First, I had

98

to do the breakfasts today (Anne's day off). I went into Mrs Elliott's room. She's almost blind and 92, but can still see colours. Her face is beautiful. It shines like the glow of a holy candle, as they say in the Apocrypha. She chuckled as she told me she'd dreamt she'd been cycling through the lanes of Essex with her sister. I try to persuade her to use the commode in her room, but she adamantly refuses, saying, "God gave me two good legs so that I should not give anyone the trouble of cleaning up after me."

I've never heard her say a bad word about anyone, but I know she's had terrific courage. Her farmhouse burnt down out in Canada three years ago. She went straight to Montreal, bought a shop, opened it as a florist, sold out in six months and then came here to be near her brother. She was 89 then!

Oh Tilly, the joy that we feel from being in her presence. She exudes love. When we kiss each other goodnight she gives me a hug and I could only wish that everyone had a Mrs Elliott to listen to their problems and give them the advice that she gives to me. She's always got one of the cats on her lap, whether on the lawn or in the house. She told me that when she was a little girl and their cat had kittens she used to spend her pocket money on different coloured ribbons, and made bows to put around the kittens' necks when they were ready to leave the mother. Then she went from house to house asking people to give one a home. She never failed to find a home for them. She saw a pig being slaughtered when she was 13 years old and has refused ever since to touch meat. She owned fruit farms, first in Essex, later in Canada; which reminds me, an absent-minded guest asked her why she went to Canada.

She told the guest, "George and I married once the First World War was over and we invested all our money in a fruit farm. When it came to harvesting the fruit the men took the day off to go to the races. During harvesting George said, 'We've kept them in a job throughout the year and now they've let us down at the most important time. We'll sell out and go to Canada.' "

They prospered in Canada and she had one child in her 40's. He was to die of a brain tumour in his 40's. The absent-minded guest listening said, "You shouldn't have been running a farm. It's not a woman's business. What would you know about running a farm?"

"Mrs Elliott knows much more about running a farm than any of us here Mrs Edwards, and she'd probably run this place much better than me. Come, I'd like advice from both of you. What shall I prepare for pudding tomorrow?" I said. They both suggested various puddings, and so bad arguments were avoided.

Mrs Elliott would have walked away but Mrs Edwards would have pressed on although she hadn't a clue what she was talking about. This brings me to another matter, and that is judging people. If someone is tall, well dressed and well spoken everyone assumes he is clever, important, capable, responsible, or an authority in some important field, although he may be as daft as a brush, as the old saying goes. It's also true that people coming upon a group of old people usually mistakenly think, 'poor old people', and behave as if the people have lost their mental faculties. This is the result of ignorance, stupidity, or lack of empathy. The old person is still the same young person inside, with a storehouse of knowledge, unless they have a disease that effects their memory (which accounts for approximately one third of our guests not being able to live alone). Two thirds are here because physically they can't cope.

Now to tell you about the wedding. A few months back, Jim's friend, Graham Watts, invited us to his daughter's wedding. Although Jim hates dressing up with top hat and tails, he agreed it would give us a break if we got someone to take charge. Mentioning this to a social worker friend who was spending the evening with us, we were delighted and surprised when she insisted that she ran it from the Friday night until the Monday morning. The Monday before the wedding, however, I received a lengthy letter from her explaining that she'd been hasty in making the decision, but found that the very idea of touching old people was repulsive to her! I rang her up and told her that I'd assumed she'd had some training as a nurse. She said she hadn't, so I rang off and remembered two dear nieces of a guest who helped decorate the Christmas trees. I rang them after I rang the local policeman's wife. The three of them agreed to look after the people while we went to the wedding.

Jim booked a taxi as he said he wouldn't be able to drive after drinking, and we booked into the hotel and then continued to the church for the wedding, and after to Graham's lovely house, where a marquee had been erected in the grounds. His daughter had married the son of a French couple who owned a farm, but could not speak English. The never-ending queue of guests, us among them, wended their way through the marquee shaking hands with the bridal couple and relations. The champagne flowed and we enjoyed ourselves as we talked to friends we hadn't seen for years, or were introduced to business acquaintances of Graham's of whom we had heard but not met. At 5 pm we returned to the hotel, as we had arranged for our friends, Alison and John, to join us there for dinner.

It was lovely to feel that I didn't have to make excuses half way through the dinner to attend to someone for once, and we all had a very merry evening until 11 pm. As we were about to say 'goodnight' in the foyer, the French Mama and Papa entered. Recognising us their faces lit up. "Ah Monsieur. Ah Madame!" We introduced our friends, and invited them to join us for a drink, so we continued to celebrate until 1 am.

Jim interpreted while John, Alison and myself desperately sought to remember the French of our school days, but eventually the time came to say 'goodnight'. Mama and Papa followed us back into the hotel, and eventually to our bedroom looking puzzled. Jim said, "We'll see you in the morning," then there was much laughter as they explained that they hadn't thought we were staying in the hotel.

Oh, my head. It began to thump and thump. I couldn't sleep. I soon regretted sitting up until 1 am. I went to the bathroom and took two aspirins. When I returned I found Jim had got into my bed. He was fast asleep. An hour later I again went to the bathroom and returned to find Jim had woken up, changed beds, and fallen asleep. Two hours later, without a wink of sleep and a pounding hammer in my head, I went to the bathroom and took another two aspirins and returned to find a sleeping Jim in my bed again. I would have laughed, but it was too painful even to smile. At 7 am I thought I'd take a bath. That might help. We'd ordered tea for 7.30 am. Coming back at twenty past I climbed into bed and then found Jim climbing in beside me.

"I haven't been able to sleep. Twin beds aren't any good," he said, cuddling my waist.

Suddenly I screamed and screamed and screamed.

"What is it darling?" asked Jim jumping out of bed.

"My leg. Don't touch me!"

"Where?" asked Jim and put his hand on a lump the size of a tennis ball on the calf of my leg. I beat on the wall in agony with both hands shouting "No, don't touch me, don't touch me." After a few minutes the lump and pain disappeared.

"Oh, I'm sorry, darling. That's beautiful. No more pain, and even my head is beginning to ease," I said.

The chambermaid then arrived with the tea, and we sat up in bed together laughing about his attempts to get into bed with me, quite unaware I wasn't there. The next morning Mama and Papa avoided our glances.

"I wonder what's the matter with them," I whispered to Jim over breakfast. Taking a stroll in the grounds later, we came face to face with them. Jim wished them a good morning and hoped they'd had a better night than I had, and explained that I'd been unable to sleep and then had an attack of cramp. They were convulsed with laughter, as they told us they thought Jim was committing some terrible offence on me when they heard me screaming "Don't touch me!"

That wedding won't be forgotten. We spent the rest of the day reading all the Sunday papers. When I was young my father used to say, "Read every paper, not one, and before you make your mind up remember they're written by men, not God." I enjoy the *Express*, followed by the *Telegraph*. The rest I read, but don't enjoy.

I must go round and say 'goodnight' to everyone now. I'll ring next week.

Much love,
Lillian.

My dear Tilly,

This will annoy you as much as it did us. We had a visitor who said she had heard we ran a very good home, and asked if I would attend a conference to be held on old people by the Mental Health Society. I was pleased and thought this would mean a day in London. How nice to hear that people appreciate our efforts! So I went cock-a-hoop to London and listened to doctors and various people lecture on the care of the elderly in nursing homes and rest homes. Most of the people attending were the owners of nursing homes. Only a handful had rest homes.

At lunch time a buffet meal of a very high standard was provided, and then the lectures were resumed. A doctor talked about rest homes and then asked me if I had any comments to make on rest homes. I stood up and said I thought that with the growing numbers of elderly people, what was wanted was not large rest homes or small ones, but a lot more rest homes catering for between 12 and 20 people where they lived as a family and were free to entertain their visitors from 7 am until midnight if necessary.

Suddenly a great clapping of hands and stamping of feet began at the back of the hall and they kept trying to drown my words, chanting "You work for reward! You work for reward"

"What do *you* work for? My reward pays your wages, and I do *work* unlike you," I told them. They kept on and on until I sat down.

A man rose and said he was the chairman of an old people's association, and that many of his members were in homes where the owners had taken a job to support the old people who had lived with them for years, and whose money had not been sufficient to enable them to pay any cost of living increases. I came back and sat and wept when I told Jim about those sick political social workers who tried to denigrate and harass me.

Maybe there are people making a fat living somewhere out of looking after the elderly. I haven't met any yet, but I'll tell you one thing. None of those who behave like that would do anything for old people or young. They are just talkers, and another thing, if they stopped giving so-called rewards to the matrons and wardens of local authority homes many would stop work and close down.

What a great evil Marx brought into this world! Myself, I would be delighted to export all those who believe in Communism to Russia permanently, where women are treated like cattle when they're expecting a child; all lined up naked and not allowed to have husbands or friends in the hospital while the baby is being born. I've seen the women repairing the roads and buildings in Gdynia looking sullen and unhappy, whereas those who preach Communism in this country just create envy.

I've got over it now, but I shall not easily forget it. But wait, one day the people who preach this doctrine will regret it. You only have to look round and see what's happening in our society and the rest of the world. Children are being encouraged to be dishonest and disruptive. They are now being deprived of their heritage — the innocence which is their right, the love of God, the teachings of Christ which have produced love and happiness throughout nearly 2,000 years.

I've often dreamt that 10 year olds are running the country, and you will see that the violence committed by 10 year olds in years to come will be on such a scale that it will mean my dreams have come true.

I will tell you one dream I have kept having this year, and that is that Jeremy Thorpe and his wife are isolated and camping on the top of Snowdon. I wonder what all that is about?

We've just had a dream come true that astonished us. We have a 58-year-old friend who is a lawyer named Eric and two years ago he married for the second time — a 30-year-old girl, named Jane. Six months ago, twice in one week, I dreamt the same dream and Jim dreamt exactly the same dream that week. Jane was removed to a mental hospital in the dream. We watched them unlocking and locking doors behind her as two nurses led her through the hospital. I recorded them, plus another dream in the same week in which Eric was driving me along a dark country road. He stopped the car in the dark, got out to spend a penny, and rolled to the bottom of the embankment. He was terribly drunk.

Three weeks ago he was over the moon with excitement, as Jane had given birth to a baby the week before, and he was looking forward to her bringing the baby home from the nursing home. A nanny had been installed and was waiting. Ten days ago he came here in despair. Jane had had to be removed to a mental hospital. He had returned home from the office the second day after Jane's homecoming and was told that the dog had worried the baby like a doll, so he had the dog shot. The next day Jane complained to him that the gardener had picked the baby up and that she had been just in time to prevent him breaking the baby's arm. The third day, when he stepped into the house it was just in time to prevent her murdering the Nanny.

A few nights ago I had a phone call from a friend of theirs whom I'd never met, asking for my advice. He said that he thought Eric was drinking too much with all the worry that he was going through and, knowing I was a friend, asked what advice I could give to help him wean Eric off the bottle.

"He's an adult used to holding his liquor. I would leave things alone, you'll only cause embarrassment for him and yourself," I advised.

"But you don't understand. Jane has always complained about him getting drunk. She said he often stops on the way home at night to spend a penny and ends up at the bottom of the embankment because he is too drunk to keep his balance."

We discussed the situation for a few minutes longer and then I hung up. Jim and I stared at each other. I said "How? Why? It's six months since the dreams. You're no longer sceptical".

"I must agreee that the number of dreams that come true are too high to be a matter of coincidence," said Jim.

Before I finish I will move on to another subject — birthdays. We always ensure that guests have a card, present and birthday cake. Very often it is their relatives who supply a very highly decorated oblong cake of magnificent proportions and ask us to cut it up and share it between guests and staff. This we do at 4 pm and all sing 'Happy birthday to you. Recently this tradition was broken in a rather expensive tradition for us.

The daughter of a padre's widow asked if she could hold a party for her mother in the hall at 7.15 pm. We agreed.

"Now about the cake," she began. I said if she wished I could order it.

"Oh good, and I should think most of the guests like sweet sherry, perhaps a couple of bottles of Bristol Cream and a couple of bottles of dry sherry. Do you think that will be enough?" asked the dotty daughter. We assured her that it would be enough and the next day collected the sherry and ordered the cake.

A week later everyone gathered in the lounge when they had finished the meal and dotty daughter rushed round with her husband and handed us all drinks then proceeded to cut the cake and distribute it. One hour later dotty daughter called for silence saying, "I'm sure that most of you, like Mummy, want to see your favourite programme on television, so I think it's time to say 'goodnight'. But first I'm sure that you'll all join me in giving a vote of thanks to the Commander and his wife for giving Mummy this splendid birthday party." Tilly, we just stared at each other. What could we say? She'd neatly turned the tables so that she didn't have to foot the bill! Fortunately a third of the guests would not remember, but I wondered how many of the others thought they didn't get a cocktail party for their birthday. It seems funny now and I'll be a bit more careful in future.

Now it's time to say 'goodnight'. We'll look forward to your phone call.

Love,

Lillian.

4th AUGUST, 1969

Dear Tilly,

It's good to be alive. I've had a very lucky escape. Jim bought me a new calor gas cooker, and the cook asked me to teach her how to make bread, which I did last Friday. At 10.30 am I left the kitchen, telling the cook that I would be back when the dough had risen, and would show her how to do the re-kneading and put the bread in tins to rise. I did this and when all the tins were put out and covered with clean tea towels in the warm to rise, I said "We can't use the Rayburn because the dinner is inside, so put the calor gas on now cook, and at maximum. Bread needs a very hot oven. I'll be back when it's time to put the loaves in the oven."

When they had risen beautifully, I said to cook, "Whip an egg in the cup, and you can brush it on the tops now, before you put the loaves in the oven," and, walking over to the new oven, I saw it was switched off.

"You never lit the gas, cook."

"I did".

"You didn't, it's stone cold and switched off."

"But I did," she declared angrily.

I grabbed the electric lighter, switched on, knelt down and put my head in the oven and BANG! All I remember thinking was, "Dear God, I didn't know I was going to die like this."

I opened my eyes and everything seemed strange. Then Jim's face came into focus, and I could hear Jenny crying. I was covered in anti-burn cream. My glasses had saved my sight. Apparently the blast hurled me straight across the table, and another working surface. The table had a rack for choppers and knives, which had damaged my back, badly bruising it. The kitchen was 40 feet long and, Jenny, standing 20 feet away, had got burnt up her arms. Fortunately, the windows were all open or I'd have probably died. The cook was far away from the blast and not in the direct line, but she couldn't find the egg or brush. Cook had lit the gas, but Jenny, as usual, dabbing away at the stoves and working surfaces, had dabbed the switch off again. The windows being open, one couldn't smell the gas!

The news travelled like wild fire. People phoned and came in to see if I was all right, and then told us awful tales about people who'd been blown up as a result of using calor gas.

One guest said, "Poor Fanny Craddock and her husband suffered from a calor gas explosion on their boat."

Another told us of a couple of friends on a caravan holiday. The

106

calor gas caught fire. The husband ran for water and couldn't open the door when he got back, and his poor wife lost her life.

Rose said one of the villagers returned home from a day's work, lit a match, and went straight through the kitchen wall, due to the pressure from the calor gas building up all day, as a result of the tap being left on.

Oh dear, Tilly, what awful tales. Jenny's arms are nearly better, but now Jim is constantly popping to the kitchen to make sure the gas taps are turned off.

Last Wednesday was a day to be remembered. The temperature was over 90°. Mr Shalk always collects bits of twigs after breakfast, and sets a fire in the hall ready for him to put some logs on and light at 6 pm, so the guests who don't want to look at television can enjoy a log fire. Naturally, this only occurs when the weather is cool. However, last Wednesday we found the log fire blazing at 10 am on a day when we were nearly all passing out.

"You've lit the fire, Mr Shalk. Why?" I asked.

"All the radiators are off," he informed me.

"But it's boiling hot, Mr Shalk. It doesn't affect hot water. There are seven immersion heaters, plus the water from the Rayburn." When he went in for coffee I removed the logs!

All the guests and staff watched the landing on the moon by Armstrong and Aldrin on the Monday, and sat around in the shade on Wednesday discussing it.

The Colonel said it was a terrific achievement for the Americans; that they were a great people, and he hoped that this would result in Russia taking a more respectful view of the Americans.

Mr McGregor said "They won't have any more problems with the Russians because they will know now that the Americans can drop a bomb on them."

"Listen to that old fool," said the Colonel to the padre.

Mrs Hart said, "It's an amazing achievement. Who would have thought in our lifetime that we'd live to hear of men walking on the moon?"

"Did they fly there?" said bewildered Mrs Raidell, and the Colonel tapped the padre's hand.

"Yes," and then quietly, "Poor soul doesn't know who she is half the time."

Old Mr Banks said he didn't see anything wrong with Communism, that it would spread throughout the world and all men would be equal, and if he hadn't belonged to a union he wouldn't have had a pension that enabled him to live here.

The Colonel fixed him with an angry blue eye. "Claptrap, utter claptrap. Have you ever been abroad?" Old Banks shook his head.

"I never wanted to; just to see a lot of foreigners with dirty habits. Give me England".

The Colonel retorted, "If I could arrange it, I'd remove everyone like you, who thinks Communism means equality, behind the iron curtain where you could all damn well enjoy your so-called equality. The West has many faults, but you only get freedom under a Western democracy. What say you Major?".

"I agree, but it's too hot for a discussion on politics, and we'll soon be living in another dimension and looking at the horrors still to come before people come to their senses."

The Colonel shook his head, lit another cigarette, and then, addressing the major, said, "Look at Masaryk. He saw what a terrible mistake Communism was. He jumped out of the window and killed himself."

"I suspect he was thrown out of the window. You are right when you say that the Americans are fine people, but I think they have a lot of very 'unfine' people to cope with, and this is a problem that's universal. Where's Anne with the tea? I'm thirsty", the Major said.

Anne appeared with a few letters and handed them to me saying, "Ah, sure, 'tis the second post has come." I handed two to the guests and then called Jim who was clipping the grass.

"Look, what's this? It's stamped, it's open, and only the name of the house is on it." We withdrew the letter and recognised old Bank's handwriting. It said:

"Dear Commander,

Did you know old people liked meat and greens instead of turnips every day, and could we all have high tea at half past five? It's too late to eat at seven o'clock."

We were speechless. After a few minutes I said, "I'll ring his son," which I duly did. I explained what had happened, and the son said he would come with his sister and wife at seven-thirty.

Tilly, they were furious with him. They said he'd complained for two years that he'd only got turnips to eat, and they had said to him, "We've seen the meals Anne takes in. Why are you the odd one out? We don't believe it."

"If he'd behaved himself he could have been living with us. He's impossible," said the daughter-in-law, and proceeded to tell us some of the naughty tricks he'd pulled on them.

They gave him a ticking off about the letter, and we felt sorry for them when they said that which ever one visited him they always had to phone the other on return, because to get sympathy the old man used to play one off against the other.

It's the same story for another guest here, Mrs Cane. She'll say to me either her daughter or her son said she must have this or ought to have that and when they visit she tells them I said they ought to buy her this, or do that, so they also phone each other and check after a visit.

Oh, Tilly, I do hope we won't be a problem to anyone if we should grow old. Last Tuesday I dreamt Mrs Phillips said she was sick and would I hold her head.

At 11 pm on Wednesday night she came to me and said she felt sick. I held her head until midnight and then phoned the doctor. He said he was off duty but if it continued after another two hours to phone his partner, but I didn't like to do that because he'd had three coronaries, so I sat all night with her, and phoned him at 6 am. He arrived, gave her an injection, and after advising an egg and jelly diet, said he'd come back in a couple of days.

Her niece visited her, and I told her that we couldn't understand the reason for her sickness.

"I'm not surprised, considering the amount of sweet stuff Auntie eats," she said.

"How do you mean?"

"Well, I bring her four boxes of chocolates, two packets of biscuits, 14 tins of cream and 14 tins of fruit every fortnight."

I checked this out with the staff, who assured me that she ate a tin of cream and fruit every morning at 11 am, so I told the niece that she couldn't have it in the future — just the odd box of chocolates and biscuits. Every day she leaves food on her plate, and will say to the other guests, "I don't know how you can eat that."

"I had Auntie for a month, and the way she ordered the children about was intolerable. I call her Aunty as a matter of respect. My father was a second cousin, but I'll see that the fruit and cream is cut out," the niece promised. I've just had a thought. When she came here they told me that she only had 10 shillings pocket money, and wouldn't even be able to afford more than £10 per week, so how is it that she's been spending at least a couple of pounds a week!

Well, that's life, Tilly, the longer we live the more we realise we know so little.

Looking forward to your phone call on Sunday.

Love,

Lillian.

Dear Tilly,

I was delighted with your story about the two Irish women who used to meet every night in the little snug bar for women 50 years ago. I can just picture the scene when the first said, "I haven't felt well all the week," and the other said, "Perhaps you're pregnant. It's three years since the last child."

"Of course I'm not pregnant!"

"How can you be sure? What are you taking?"

"Oh, don't be stupid, oi don't take nothing, for doesn't the silly old fool come home plastered every night, and when he attempts it in the morning don't I say to him 'Sure and haven't ye had enough? You've kept me up half the night and oi've got to get the children off to school. Ye've got it on the brain, man'. Sure the silly old fool never remembers."

I must tell you something funny. We have a guest, Mrs O'Shea, who is very absent-minded. She sprained her ankle when she was out walking. The doctor said, "Keep her in bed till the swelling goes down" and this created a problem as she never keeps still. Jim, the staff and myself popped backwards and forwards to the downstairs flat where Mrs O'Shea had a room, and constantly put her back into bed. This continued for a week. Mrs O'Shea had a peculiar habit. She always greeted people by raising her right arm right up and her right foot a little. It looked very odd.

After a week the doctor said she could get up. Back in the office Jim said, "Now you've got another problem. She has already forgotten that she's supposed to get up." I went back and asked her to dress. Half an hour later I sent Anne over. She was still in bed. Half an hour after that Jim said, "You'll have to dress her for the first couple of days," so I went back prepared to dress her, but, as I opened her door, Anne told me, "You're wanted on the telephone."

"Mrs O'Shea, look. You start getting dressed dear. There are your shoes to put on," I said, handing them to her.

Replacing the telephone, I said to Jim, "I can hear the laundry van coming up the back drive," and we both drew the bolts of the double back doors to enable the laundry man to carry the baskets through. As he stepped down from the driver's seat Mrs O'Shea stepped out of the back door into the drive with just her shoes on, and saluted the laundry man with her usual curious wave! I hurried her back to the room and dressed her, but we'll always remember the laundry man's face. It was a picture.

I've torn the tendon in my leg and I'm hopping round temporarily on a zimmer. I did the same thing a week before we went on the *Misteria*, so I was limping at the time I had that awful experience on the camel, when the driver threatened to make it race if I didn't pay them more money.

Miss Osborne has given me two exquisitely embroidered and beaded cushions she has just finished. Last year a 97-year-old guest gave me a tapestry cushion when she had finished it. It's a work of art. How wonderful to produce such works of art at that age! I used to knit and embroider reasonably well, but I could never have produced work like this. I had to give that up in my 20s due to the agony I suffered the next day from inflamed nerves that passed between my two extra ribs. Funny that, Tilly, that people are born with extra ribs, toes or fingers. After listening to a debate in Parliament we know that there is one blessing, and that is that people aren't born with an extra tongue!

When I was saying 'goodnight' to Mrs Elliott last night she talked about London 70 years ago, when she was manageress of four restaurants. She said how good it was now that one didn't see old ladies poverty stricken and wearing men's boots, often with the uppers coming away from the soles. She described the life and times vividly to me and then asked me if Miss Osborne had made a mistake when she'd told her that today you have to be careful to lock your doors and windows, because if squatters get in you can't get them out unless you go to law.

"That's quite true. The only people who are protected are top civil servants, and also council house tenants — as far as I'm aware," I told her. She was shocked.

"But that's unjust. Two people are earning the same money; one may squander it and the other try to make a good home for his wife and family, but they could still suffer extreme hardship. I don't understand it," she said.

"Well, life has always been unjust for some and always will be. All we can do is pray that justice will prevail some day. Not all people are as good as you, and you must not worry at your age."

"Happiness for me is having you here to talk to and to kiss goodnight and to listen to. It's in relationships and not possessions. They tie us down." She squeezed me tight and kissed me goodnight, and laughed when I assured her that all pussies were safely bedded for the night. She did love cats. If she had her eyesight she wouldn't be with us as she's as capable and efficient as she was 70 years ago.

Having written this I'm now off to decorate one of the bathrooms. I make a list each New Year of the jobs to be done, as does Jim, and we are usually able to get the list ticked off by the time December comes around. There are only two more rooms to be decorated this year unless someone else leaves the plug in the bath or basin!

Look forward to your next letter.

Much love,
Lillian.

My dear Tilly,

Like you we had an endless supply of green beans and, three times a week, half a dozen of the guests sliced them for us for lunch, and we gave away beans to staff and friends nearly every day. The asparagus bed and the artichokes flourished well. The one disappointment Jim had was that after having successfully got a row of morning glory to bloom, he went out one morning and found that Mrs Faile, who has always claimed to be a keen gardener, had cut them all down, as she thought they were weeds. She'd also uprooted and burnt the six prize chrysanthemums we'd had given to us for a present.

Last year we had the crazy-paved area outside the kitchen, about 15 feet square, a mass of aubretia. Everyone praised it. It was magnificent. While we were out one morning earlier this year, before it bloomed, we returned to find an energetic 65 year old Mrs Faile, complete with gardening gloves, standing with the wheelbarrow in front of the house beaming.

"I've always been a keen gardener. Now is the time to pull the weeds before they get a strong hold," she announced. Jim came in 10 minutes later in despair.

"The blasted woman has undone three years work. Every bit of the aubretia has been pulled out," he said. I commiserated with him and cheered him up.

"It's no use wasting time in regrets. We'll have to take care and point out to her what is not to be touched if she gets in the mood to garden again," I said.

The other week she stormed down the stairs waving a daily paper.

"Look at this. It's disgusting. They're making fun of Mr. Wilson. We ought to do something about it," she said angrily. Jim gently told her that satire is a healthy thing, and that all politicians have been satirised.

That reminds me of the last election. Two of the guests' relatives, at different times, suggested to Jim that, as a third of the guests were absent-minded, he could ensure that their cross was put in the right box! Jim didn't waste much breath in telling them what he thought of them, and it led to us discussing how many people who suffered from arterio-schlerosis were influenced either by families, or by the managers, owners, or staff where they lived. Obviously there are people in positions of authority who, like Jim, wouldn't dream of using their position to interfere with the unalienable right of a person to put his cross where he wishes, rightly or wrongly, but the very fact

*Thanks to my willing guest, three years
hard work was now in my wheelbarrow!*

that two people suggested this, means that there must be more people
like them in all parties, who if given the opportunity, would try to
influence people to rig the postal votes.

Again, if it was done on a wide scale, I ask myself if it would not
mean that maybe the votes cancelled each other out? Oh, for my
childhood's faith and trust! In God it has not diminished; only in
people. The more I discover about people the more I know that it is
only by continually attempting to reach up to the teachings of Christ,
and put them into practice, that one is saved from despair. I have

probably got more faults that I find in others, but thank God I have always too much to do to worry about how I'm going to explain my angers and faults when I pass over.

It will soon be time to put the clocks back. Few people remember the adage "Spring forward and Fall back", but it reminds me of last Spring. Jim put all the clocks forward, and I, for some unknown reason, decided to do the same thing, and some event took place that made me forget to tell him what I'd done.

I got up and found the staff downstairs, although it wasn't quite daylight! We prepared the breakfasts, sent them around the rooms, and then discovered that everyone had been woken far too soon, I heard nothing all day after but, "I feel tired." "I could go back to bed." I won't touch the clocks again. It was the talking point for a week.

We had a surprise this week as a result of a firm of accountants phoning us and asking if we could get Mrs Vale, a guest who has been here nine years, to answer their letters. Mrs Vale is a very quietly spoken and genteel woman. When we were going on our first holiday she sent for me to tell me she was worried because her money had been invested badly by the bank manager, and she couldn't afford the fees any longer.

I assured her that she hadn't any worry, and I would discuss it when we got back from holiday. Meanwhile she could check with the bank manager how much was left, so that it could be put into an annuity. When we returned from our holiday she said the bank manager had said there was only £4,000 left.

"Well, that's easy. Invest £3,000 in an annuity, leaving yourself something to fall back on," I advised. I also reminded her that we might not always be around, and if she moved to another home she'd need the money the annuity would bring in.

"Oh, no. I could never do that. I want to leave the money to my nephew," she replied.

"In that case, we'll be sorry to lose you, so you had better make arrangements to live with your nephew," I said.

A week later she sent for me and gave me a cheque, and assured me that from now on she would be able to pay all her bills. I asked her to write to the accountants and told her that they said it was a matter of urgency. She said that they'd never written to her.

"That's not true. I sort the post and I often send one over with the postmark, which I recognise as coming from them," I said.

She swore she'd never had the letters, so I questioned Anne who took them over. It turned out that one week she'd get Anne to draw her pension and put it in a Post Office account in the village, and the next week she got Mai to withdraw it, but put it in a Post Office account in the next village.

I passed this knowledge back to the accountants, and it turned out that a padre's widow had been paying our fees into her account for 18 months, since she'd told her that she was destitute. We contacted her bank manager who confirmed that she had £4,000 left, and that the reason she had lost a lot of money was due to lending it to a relative to start a business, and he'd gone bankrupt!

When it's Derby Day we always have a sweepstake for the guests and staff, to give them an interest in watching the race, and Mrs Vale has always refused to buy a shilling ticket because, as she said, "I'm a Methodist, and I don't believe in gambling. It's evil. It leads to people lying, cheating, and keeping their families short of money instead of leading a good Christian life."

What a disappointment she's turned out to be! Naturally, nobody else knows this, except the accountants, bank manager and ourselves. Anne and Mai aren't bright enough to wonder why she keeps two Post Office accounts. The rest of the guests say "Isn't she brave?" or Isn't she a lady?" or "Isn't she a good Christian?"

Money is the one thing people rarely tell you the truth about, and it's the same today as it has been since money was first invented. It's often the people with the most money who lie about it, and are the meanest. To us it just shows how stupid, ignorant and impoverished they are.

I heard gales of laughter coming from the linen room. I investigated and joined in when Rose told me that Anne handed cook a letter saying, "Ah sure, here's another envelope from the Fylde Coast. Do you suppose you've won again?"

Cook opened it. It was £100 from "ERNIE". She'd won £50 in each of the previous two months.

"Sure now, you'll be wanting to celebrate when we return from Mass on Sunday night. Sure and you're the lucky one!"

"We won't be celebrating. 'Tis very unlucky to share one's winnings. Did ye not know that?" said cook. That was a sharp remark!

We must soon paint the great hall. Jim will use a paint brush for the ceilings, windows, columns and skirtings, and I'll use a roller on the walls. It's a big job and I'll be glad when its over.

Will phone on Sunday.

Much love,
Lillian.

3rd NOVEMBER, 1970

Dear Tilly,

I had a shock a couple of weeks ago. You remember way back a couple of years, when I employed bouncing, hard-working Katy as a result of being on friendly terms with the brother of a guest who was a doctor at the hospital for subnormal people? Well, during the last three months, Katy had become very argumentative with Anne. It got so bad I rang the social worker who introduced her to us in the first place.

"I'm sorry, but she's been with you almost two years. Once a patient is out of the hospital for over six months they're referred to the local authorities," she said. "I will arrange for one of their social workers to call. The realisation that she will lose the freedom that she has enjoyed may bring her to her senses."

She's free from lunchtime each day and works from 5.30 pm until seven. I've saved half her salary for her as I opened a Post Office savings book in her name when she started, arranged her holidays, and she now has a large wardrobe stacked with clothes, so I can't understand what's got into her.

She'd had 10 illegitimate babies before she came to us; one had been adopted and was now in care! All the others were subnormal and she had been cured of VD.

The doctor who arranged her employment said, "It's an offence for a man knowlingly to have sex with a subnormal person, but most of the pregnancies were due to relationships within the hospital." He had warned me that I would have to keep an eye on what she got up to in her free time.

I arranged that she took her days off with Anne who is very devout, and she spent the evenings looking at television or on the lawn with the staff in the summer.

A fortnight ago a young 22-year-old social worker arrived and, when Katy was asked why she shouted at Anne, she said, "Because she only waits on table. I have to clean the dining room."

She was wrong. Jenny always cleaned it. Katy continued to cry and said, "I can never go out on my own. I always have to go with Anne."

"Katy it's for your own good," I interrupted. "You don't want to end up being parted from another baby do you?"

"Do you mind, Mrs Mannooch?" said the social worker. Katy is entitled to sex as much as you or I. Come along Katy. Pack your things. You're coming with me."

Tilly, I was mad! I felt like saying, "You should be made to rear all the subnormal children that Katy and other poor souls like her bring into this world. You should be cleaning them and changing them, not giving stupid advice."

We thought we'd seen the back of poor Katy, but no. Last week I went into the kitchen at 6 pm to find Katy sobbing loudly and telling the staff that she had to work before she went to her job and when she returned at night. She complained she had to pay the hostel and her fares to work, and hadn't got enough to last her for cigarettes. What was worse, she'd come by taxi and hadn't got any money to pay the fare. I told her that only the social worker could arrange for her to get her job back here and paid the taxi driver to take her back.

Tilly, what is going to happen to the world? We're between armies of permissive social do-gooders, armies of extremists, armies of drug pushers and takers. Scientifically, we have made great progress in the Western World, but morality, truthfulness and commonsense have been thrown out of the window. I foresee the day when youngsters will be corrupted and violent unless governments wake up and take action in time to prevent a catastrophe.

There isn't any such thing as Utopia. When I was younger it used to puzzle me why governments in other Christian countries allowed brothels. Today, I see with sadness, it was to protect women — but this reminds me of an incident which made Jim laugh.

After the war I spent a night in Paris when returning from Bordeaux. I arose early and thought I would do some shopping before catching the train to return to England. Before the shops opened I strolled along, wending my way through hundreds of women pacing up and down outside the shops. I thought there must be a sale on. The women didn't look very friendly towards me and I began to be very embarrassed. No less than half a dozen men propositioned me within 10 minutes, so I approached the Gendarme and complained. He roared with laughter as he explained that the brothels were closed and I'd joined the queue! I felt a fool and, after making a couple of purchases, rushed off to wait for the train.

I had another embarrassing moment when I stayed at a hotel in Pouillac, outside Bordeaux. The hotel had been occupied by the Germans during the war and the French owners, with a teenage son and daughter, were very kind people. He'd fought with the French Resistance while she had worked from dawn until midnight in fear that the children would be removed from her.

I was sitting writing cards while waiting for my husband, when about 20 Americans who had just stepped ashore off a Liberty boat, walked towards me. Suddenly, I heard a deep Texan drawl, "Gee, Frenchy, here's a bit of all right. Chat her up and find out what she

118

charges. Just look at those tits. Go on Frenchy, chat her up." My legs, waist, hair were all duly remarked on. I kept on writing as they began to gather round. Jacques rushed out and told them not to speak to Madame, that I was English and his guest.

Were their faces red! Two nights later I was still waiting for my husband while reading in the bedroom when Jacques rushed in and, grabbing hold of me, took me to his bedroom and locked me in with his wife and children. The Americans had got drunk, and one had thrown himself out of a window. The police arrived quickly and order was restored.

Will phone at the weekend.

Love,
Lillian.

Tilly my dear,

I'm glad you were warm and comfortable throughout the snow. It must be terrible for the old and disabled if they're living on their own when the weather is so dreadful. I'm sure there are many people who watch over neighbours when we get such bad weather; perhaps someday, even if not in our lifetime, there will come a time when nobody will suffer from loneliness and cold. Yet I'm afraid if we get to Utopia we might find greater evils.

As you know, we finished the hall, working flat out the whole week. I gave it four coats. It looks delightful, despite a setback caused by the snow. There's a small hole in the attic leading across the rafters to an open lead-lined gutter that runs through the attic. No one could get through it except me, because, although I'm amply padded, I've got very small bones. The ice had set into blocks three feet long and six inches square right through. If there was a quick thaw it would have meant the ceilings might come down over the north wing, so I had to ease myself through and remove each block of ice, lying on my tummy, and pass them back through the hole, where Jim passed them to the four staff with buckets. It took from nine o'clock to 12.30 in the morning to clear it.

At six o'clock the following night I heard a guest calling me urgently in the hall.

"Quick, the water is coming down the wall behind the piano", she said. With lamps and chisels and buckets we had to work on the balconies as there came a quick thaw. The water, being unable to get out over the concrete balconies in time, had escaped down inside the house.

When we finally bathed and changed it was 10 o'clock, and Jim was glad of a gin and tonic, and myself of a sherry. We sat and talked about the possibilities of anything else going wrong, but hoped it wouldn't. Tap! Tap! Tap! "Oh, no, not again," we thought, and looked into the hall. There was nothing alarming to be seen, but the tapping still persisted.

"You check one half of the building and I'll check the other. We needn't worry about the north wing. That tapping is too close."

Within minutes I'd found it. Someone had left the bath taps on and the plug in place in the bathroom! An hour later we sat down and discussed the repairing of the ceiling of the room underneath. We removed the guest to our dressing room. After all this I felt as if I'd qualified as a plumber's mate.

The next morning we were having breakfast when we heard Rose calling us urgently.

"The water is rushing like mad in the bathroom next to Mrs Drake's room and she won't open the door," said Rose.

"Quick! get the buckets," I said, as I hammered on the door and pleaded with dear old Mrs Drake to come out. She did, poor soul, her face covered with lather, as she'd been about to shave. The water was cascading through the edges of a cupboard that had been stupidly nailed across the tank. Jim got tools and a ladder, and Rose caught as much water as she could, and I tipped the buckets in the bath.

Having finished in the bathroom Jim rang the builders and got it put right. Rose said, "No wonder they had one man working full time on the roof in the olden days."

"Yes, and that was before they even had tanks and baths here. They employed 15 gardeners and 25 staff to look after one person here. They needed them for all the fires, laundry and cleaning," I reminded her. Well, the wall in the hall dried out without leaving a mark, thank heaven. Now the bad weather has improved we hope for a quiet and uneventful period, especially after the last two days.

I told you that we have very rich neighbours and that the wife was an alcoholic. The day before yesterday she said to her gardener, "Go and cut those blackberry plants down in the next garden. They're coming over our fence." He did, as the owners were in London. Later, I got a phone call asking me if I could invite them over and make the peace when they came back from London, as the husband knew they had been in the wrong. I didn't want to get involved, but eventually decided to heal the breach and walk over to see them. I explained that she'd been tight, and now was embarrassed. They said they were cultivated blackberries, and that they were furious when they found a note from their daily help telling them about it, but they were very understanding when I left, and peace was restored.

The next day, in gratitude, he said he was going into the great metropolis (meaning the nearest town) for an hour, and did I want to come. Jim said "We need bird seed and fish food for the aquarium in the hall," (which reminds me, you said you are thinking of getting tropical fish. Don't forget that, when we had the great power cut, we had to ensure that the temperature of the water stayed the same all night so that we didn't lose the fish). I took advantage of the offer and he dropped me off at the pet shop, arranging to pick me up outside Marks & Spencers half an hour later.

There was a marvellous St Bernard in the pet shop, and we made a fuss of each other. Alas, when I stepped out of the shop I put my foot up to the ankle in the largest lump of St Bernard you can visualise. Did I feel awful? I limped down the street, bought newspaper and made for the nearest toilets. I washed the shoe and removed the tights. Eventually, I wrapped the washed shoe in clean newspaper, and walking (or rather, limping) with one bare foot, met our neighbour and asked him to put it in the boot of his Rolls Royce. In the evening, I laughed as I remembered how embarrassed I was. They say if you put your foot in it it's lucky, but I'll watch where I put my feet in future.

I overheard one of the guests say Mrs Hart was a suffragette and chained herself to the railings. The other guest said, "I couldn't stand the suffragettes. They were stupid." I thought how stupid the latter guest was. I read Lady Pethick Lawrence's *My Life in this Changing World,* and knew her sister Dorothy Pethick. Both of them suffered very much for women to have rights. Miss Dorothy Pethick had her teeth broken six times by force feeding. She was the most dignified and stoic person I've known. It was she who made me aware that a man called as a witness in court used to get paid five shillings for the day, a boy half a crown, and a woman nothing.

Tilly, we need another suffragette movement to restore respect and good manners, and prevent the purveyors of filth from flooding the world with film shows and books that exploit women and children. Unless firm action is taken God help all the people in years to come! The degradation and violence will be on a scale undreamt of in any previous age. There hasn't been anything produced in the world of art in this century that can compare with the works of artists of previous centuries, whether it is in painting, music or architecture.

I do believe that there will come a time, although not in our lifetime, when the people will worship God and look back in horror at the things that happen now, the same as one looks back in horror at many scenes described in the six volumes of Old and New London, which span the life and times of Londoners and London over hundreds of years.

Did you know that, at the beginning of the 19th century, a crossing sweeper sold the right to his pitch to sweep the road clean for what was the then fabulous sum of a thousand pounds? He always swept the filth back again to ensure he had customers! I also noticed that nearly everyone convicted of theft was executed, whereas murderers very often went free. Today, thank God, people are not executed for theft, but dangerous and horrible murderers are set free against public opinion, to commit murder again sometimes, and that is not right. We all feel that the murderer who murdered as a result of a passionate, unpremeditated quarrel should not suffer all his life in prison, as he will probably suffer enough from his conscience, but the most evil murderers only get a short sentence and are set free. Look how many murder again.

As you can see, I do manage to get some time in the evenings to read. I've read every book that has been written by Priestley, Jung, J. W. Dunne and many others who have written on time and space and dreams, but I have never read of an acceptable explanation as to why we have precognitive dreams. As the number of my recorded precognitive dreams grow year by year it only reassures me that we definitely leave our bodies when asleep.

Ah well, we'll all know the answers one day.

Goodnight, Tilly my love.

Much love,
Lillian.

Tilly dear,

I told you on the phone it was all over and done with, and that I would write and give you all the details as it happened, so here they are.

It was 11 pm and all the guests were in bed and asleep except for Major Stanley, and, as it turned out, Mrs Pryce Fleming. Major Stanley likes to watch TV until 10.30 pm or 11 pm depending on what's on. Then, when he has undressed for bed, he rings the intercom, as the red light flashes in every room. I go quickly and help him into bed and switch his intercom off. He can get out of bed himself, but not in, due to his paralysis. I was about to tuck him up and the red light flashed above his bed.

"I won't be a minute Major, I'm wanted," I said as I rushed off and up the main staircase. The control panel for the intercom was in our bedroom, which was the first door on the right of a large square landing. As I looked inside I saw the flames licking from five holes at the base of the mattress, and Jim was saying over the intercom: "What do you mean, you smelt smoke, Mrs Pryce Fleming. The bed's on fire but there's no smoke as yet anyway." I ran for the nearest fire extinguisher, a new one bought a month ago when all the others were tested. I fired it and it was empty! Someone must have deliberately emptied it, as they were tested at short and regular intervals. I rushed away and grabbed another. When the flames had disappeared we stared at each other.

"My God!" said Jim, "Look! It has been set fire to by a cigarette lighter." When I looked, I could see the long scorch marks around each hole.

"She said she had given a banana to Miss Wild next door to us, and smelt the smoke, and went back to her room to warn us, but there's no smell of smoke; a smell of wet burning bed, yes — now — but no smoke."

I crept into Mrs Wild's room. She was sound asleep. No bananas. I also checked on the residents in each room. All sound asleep. I finished tucking Major up and then Jim asked Mrs Pryce Fleming to come down to the lounge.

She stood shifting her weight from one foot to another as she lit a cigarette with the flame turned fully up almost three to four inches long. We looked at each other.

"You set fire to the bed Mrs Pryce Fleming. Your room is far away from our room. There are two smoke doors between your room and ours," said Jim. She denied it.

"You did not give Miss Wild a banana, and she's sound asleep." She insisted she did give her a banana.

"I must ask you to leave after this, so I'll say 'goodnight'," said Jim. We talked about it for five minutes and then Jim phoned her new son-in-law and asked him to remove her the following day.

"I certainly won't. I'm going to sue you for libel," he said and hung up. Jim rushed to the toilet where he vomitted dreadfully. When he recovered he phoned the police. I hadn't thought then, but, of course, Mrs Pryce Fleming had her own phone and had obviously rung her son-in-law before we did. The police arrived and, after an examination of the bed, pronounced that it had been set fire to by a lighter, but was now out.

"I'll never sleep on that bed again although it's a new one. Please put it out of the window," I insisted. They opened the windows wide and heaved it out on to the lawn. It was five minutes to midnight. They interviewed her and then told us they were convinced she'd done it, and would interview her again in the morning.

We talked with the police until 2 am and then decided to sleep, if we could, in the small bed in the dressing room. This meant we were cut off from the main intercom. We sat dismayed on the wide window sill of the dressing room and watched where the whole of the parkland seemed to be alight as a result of the bed burning away in front of the bedroom window. The fire had been smouldering inside all the time, and the wind fanned it into life. We'd have been burnt to death, and everyone in the place if I hadn't insisted on it being thrown out of the window. It had been a magnificent bed.

We tried to work out what sort of mind she had to do this. We recalled that every time she'd been invited in for a sherry, she kept telling us the same story of how in the last home the fire brigade was called by a mad old woman at 2 am, and of how she used to watch the nurse go out on the lawn with the dog at 2 am. Each time she laughed when she said she was glad the nurse got the sack.

I now realised I'd made a terrible mistake in not taking the doctor's advice. When she'd been here just a week she gave me a long list of prescriptions and had said, "Tell the doctor I want these put up."

"Certainly not. I must examine her first," said our doctor, and half an hour later he said, "Get rid of her. She's dangerous."

Oh, I'm used to dealing with people who suffer with nerves. I've been a psychiatric nurse," I said. He warned me once more. Now I know he'd recognised how dangerous she really was, and I could kick myself.

At 4 am we squeezed into the small bed, and it didn't seem as if we'd slept when the door was crashed open and half a dozen firemen towered over us.

I fled downstairs to be met by a sobbing Mai. She threw her arms around my neck and said, "I thought you and the Commander were dead, Oh dear, I thought you were dead." I hugged her and asked her what had happened. She had got up at 6 am as usual, seen the smouldering bed on the lawn, tried our door (which was locked), pulled the intercom from her room, and getting no reply, thought we were dead inside the room. She remembered Mrs Pryce Fleming was younger and usually up late, so she went to her room crying and found Mrs Pryce Fleming sitting on the bed with a glass of brandy in one hand, holding her head, and rocking backwards and forwards, saying, "I never smelled smoke". She asked her what to do, but couldn't get any sense out of her, so she phoned one of the neighbours who told her that they would call the fire brigade.

Tilly. The dream! Do you remember? I told you in 1967 that I dialled 999 at midnight, and the parkland was lit up by a big fire in front of my bedroom. It has come exactly true. Some dreams come true in weeks or months, but 1971 is four years later.

To get back to Mai. I said we'd all have a cup of tea when the fire chief, with our local constable, Joe Harris, came into the lounge. The fire chief began to lecture me on my stupidity in not calling the fire brigade the night before, but Joe Harris intervened and explained that the police had confirmed that the fire was out. He also told him about Mrs Pryce Fleming, and of how a burnt out match had been laid in the middle of the landing to make it appear as if someone had used a match to start the fire. He assured him it was done deliberately with a lighter.

After a cup of tea we got on with the usual chores, and by 9.30 am the detectives had arrived. They first questioned the staff, then Miss Wild, who swore that Mrs Pryce Fleming had never come to her room, and that she never allowed anyone to come to her room. By 11 am they had got to Mrs Pryce Fleming, and interviewed her for two hours. They told us afterwards that they knew without doubt that she had done it.

We explained that we could give her a month's notice, as the son-in-law had refused to take her away. They sympathised and said if he went ahead with the libel action they would produce evidence to prove she did it. In the evening we discussed it with friends, and they reminded us that she had made friends with Lady Dance in the next room, and that Lady Dance had pulled the intercom four times — twice when they were here last week between 10 pm and midnight — and each time I'd rushed to her room she'd complained that she'd pulled it for an hour and couldn't get an answer. The penny dropped!

Mrs Pryce Fleming had an obsession about fire and had obviously

126

impressed Lady Dance with the need to test the intercom in case of emergency. Our friends also reminded us that when we'd offered her a drink with them, that she'd repeatedly told the story of the fire in her last residence. Also they pointed out that she could have phoned her son-in-law. She had 15 minutes to do so before we phoned him.

"What would your reaction be if the owners of a home phoned you and asked you to remove your mother because she'd set fire to it?" Jim was asked.

"My God, No. How awful. What did she do?"

"Exactly!" I said. We now felt that we must arrange for her to be watched 24 hours a day until she left. The constable's wife took the midnight to 4 am shift, I took from 4 am until 8 am, and others filled in until midnight.

Lady Dance told Margaret that Mrs Pryce Fleming had been wrongfully accused of arson, and that subnormal Florrie had started the fire with a match. She'd actually seen her do it and we were wicked to accuse Mrs Pryce Fleming. Mai reported this to me and Margaret admitted it. We'd asked the staff to say nothing about it. We hadn't told the other guests, and Mrs Wild agreed to say nothing and I believe she kept her word. Our barrister friend arranged for us to see Counsel within a few days.

Oh Tilly, I never realised what that would really mean. He questioned me for over an hour as though I'd falsely accused her of arson.

"Why don't you like her? Why did you jump to the conclusion it was her? She was always offering to buy you presents, you say. Why did you refuse her? Why, why, why? Oh, my dear Tilly, you would have thought I'd made it all up, but once it was over he shook my hand, told me not to worry about her, and said he was sure everything would be all right.

"He had to question you like that," said Jim "They were the sort of questions her defence counsel would put to you."

Two days later we had an unexpected visit from the Health Department, by a strange man and the nursing officer. I took them from room to room and introduced them to any guests who were still in them. Every now and again the health officer said, "They're all so happy and comfortable. How nice to see them with animals on their laps."

"I told you so", the nurse kept repeating. We finished by introducing him to guests in the lounge, and then ordered coffee and cakes for them.

We talked about guests and staff, when he suddenly said, "May I see your menu book."

"We are not a nursing home, so by law we are not required to keep one, but as a matter of fact I do keep a list of the menus in my diary along with all the other events that take place daily here, plus my dreams every morning. I don't mind you looking." I returned with an armful of foolscap size diaries, with a full page allowed for each day. He opened one, quickly scanned some pages and said, "Remarkable! You're certainly kept busy, and your guests are very lucky to be here".

"What on earth was all that about? We've not long had the annual inspection," I said to Jim. "Mrs Pryce Fleming must have reported us through her solicitor. It's obvious she complained about the meals."

"It's stupid for them to send anyone when we've got the head man's father here. They know all about the place," I snapped back.

"Oh yes, but you don't see what officialdom is all about. Once a complaint has been made they would have to get an official who was not under any obligation to defend us," said Jim.

Three weeks of intense strain passed, and then she announced she was leaving. We received a phone call from the solicitor to say the action had been withdrawn. Myself, I couldn't understand many things about it. Why did the police never bring an arson charge, or the insurance company who paid for the bed? Before the war, insurance companies took action over arson.

I believe she was extremely wealthy, and the reason I refused her gifts were two-fold. I didn't want to be bought, or cause a guest to think that there was any favouritism. As she was only 60 years of age we felt sorry for her, and that's the reason we'd sometimes invite her to have a drink with our friends if she came to the lounge door. I think that she set fire to the bed and called us on the intercom, thinking that we would make her the heroine of the hour, and that all the guests would believe she'd saved them.

The week before all this happened we sat discussing the lease that is due for renewal next year and, as I've been doing the cooking since cook got married and moved to London, we've saved some money. Jim hopes to persuade her to sell us the freehold, as we could then lease it to the council as a permanent home for the elderly when we are too old to run it.

Will ring you on Sunday.

Much love,
Lillian.

Dear Tilly,

I told you that Miss Neal couldn't relieve us at Easter to get away for a holiday, so I rang Hilda and Justin who've been coming to dinner every few weeks for the past three years. Well, they agreed to move in with their teenage children for three weeks, so we were able to get away to Mauritius. You said you thought it must be a beautiful place from a study of the post cards we sent you. It was superb.

We left London at nine o'clock in the evening and landed for fuel at Cyprus and Nairobi, and we arrived at Mauritius four o'clock the next afternoon. We were greeted with a wax-like flamingo flower and a taxi to take us to the hotel, an hours drive away. At the hotel, which has been built in bungalow style, we had a spacious twin-bedded room with bathroom and toilet, and a patio, complete with tables and chairs, within 50 yards of the lagoon. Instead of going to the dining room for breakfast we had it served on the patio. The crested bul-buls used to fly on to the table and help themselves to our marmalade; the scarlet cardinal birds flew round us, and iguanas pressed to the trunks of trees, stretched their heads and looked at us with interest.

After breakfast we swam in the warm waters of the lagoon, and saw fish of every design and colour swimming around us in the clear waters. We went snorkelling and it was as if we'd been transported to another planet, as the colours changed. Once you're under the water they become more beautiful than one could ever imagine.

Every day the same Indian driver collected us and took us to different parts of the island. He also took us to meet his wife and children in his own immaculate house, set in a pretty garden, where the Amaryllis lilies bloomed wildly in profusion surrounding the gardens. The monkeys and their off-spring crossed the roads in front of us as we drove along, and we weren't troubled by stinging insects or snakes, because the island has remained free of them.

Mauritius was a paradise, green all the year round, and almost the same temperature. We passed through little villages where the population was Indian; the women were exquisite with beautiful features, and saris of every colour. The Chinese seemed to control the money supply and ran the casino at Port Louis. We thought Port Louis the most colourful place, especially the market with its display and luscious tropical fruits, strange fish, and every conceivable kind of merchandise. We noticed the people were proud and only one child asked for money. His grandmother promptly smacked him and said in French, "We do not beg from anyone."

One Sunday, driving along, we noticed about 150 Indians walking along a path through the sugar plantations, and asked the driver where they were going.

"To the Temple, where the Holy Men will climb a ladder of Panga knives while in a trance," was the reply. These Panga knives are what they cut the sugar cane with and are razor sharp.

"If I get permission would you like to go?" he enquired.

"Yes, of course we would love to go," I assured him.

We followed very slowly until we came to a clearing, where four men sat on the ground obviously in a trance. In front of the Temple a wooden ladder had been erected with the rungs made of 18 panga knives with the sharp edges pointing upwards. The Indians formed a circle. Nobody spoke, but an aged Indian stepped forward and, taking us to the centre, indicated that we were to test the sharpness of the knives, which we did. The sun blazed down from a deep blue sky.

There was a sudden silence as if the birds had stopped singing. Then the drums began to beat. One of the men in a trance rose and began to climb the ladder, dancing on each knife. We were within two feet, and could see he put his weight on the knives. Eventually he got to the top and descended on the other side. This performance was repeated by the other men, although they didn't descend on the other side but came straight back down. Each man was then taken into the Temple where a feast had been prepared for them. They had fasted for six weeks to prepare themselves for this breathtaking spectacle. Not a drop of blood was spilt!

We thanked the people for allowing us to see the ceremony. They were friendly and gentle. When we got back to the hotel and told the others they wished they had been with us. There were only four English people who'd landed in Mauritius with us and they seemed only to want to lounge on the beach round the boat house all day, and take part in the night life. The famous zoological gardens, with the hundred year old tortoise, provided us with another unforgettable day. The Museum of Port Louis, with its display of reconstructed Dodos (that are now extinct through man's greed and stupidity), made another interesting day.

We climbed the Pieter Both Mountain; we picked guavas and spent a day at Blue Bay. Blue Bay is incredible. Not one blue, but every shade of blue from the palest pastel colour to the deepest blue you can imagine. We could have stayed there and never got tired of it, but the day we were there was a feast day, and the black population had gathered to celebrate. They insisted that we join them, and if we hadn't been flying back the next day we would have accepted a drink, but we didn't dare risk one tot of the potent home-made rum they offered us, in case we missed the plane. The marvellous thing about Mauritius is that, having three different nationalities, each nationality celebrates not only its own feast days, but also all the others' feast days.

As usual, we did not escape an eventful holiday. We'd kept the air conditioning on and coming in from a warm night to an icy cold bedroom caused Jim to get one of the worst attacks of bronchial pneumonia I've witnessed. A French doctor arrived from Curepipe and made out a prescription for antibiotics. On the way to phone for a taxi, I met one of our English compatriots who, having heard that Jim was very ill, was adamant that she must take me to the chemist to collect the prescription. I was very grateful, but regretted it after I'd been kept waiting over an hour in the chemist while Mauritians handed over prescriptions. I noticed they got one aspirin for sixpence. When I eventually picked up the antibiotics, I got into the car, and was greeted with, "If I'd known this was going to happen I would certainly never have offered to take you." Silence reigned on the return journey.

Thanks to the antibiotics, one week later Jim was fit enough to attempt to eat a boiled egg for breakfast. The houseboy, 16 stone, 30-year-old Peter, put a small white egg in front of Jim, and mango, bacon and eggs in front of me. I said, "Peter, in England we have big, brown eggs this colour," touching his fingers. Peter spoke French, but hardly any English. Fifteen minutes later he appeared and put a plate of burnt black sausages in front of Jim, having obviously thought I meant I wanted burnt sausages.

While bathing in the lagoon, I noticed what appeared to be an extremely large sack bloated with water.

"Who threw that in here?" I asked, and couldn't get out of the water quickly enough as it rose out of the water. It was a baby manta ray that had got in through the reef. Jim thought it hilarious, but when you have to stretch the truth to claim you're five feet tall, a baby manta ray looks the size of King Kong beside you.

I used the boat house to buy a sandwich for my lunches, while Jim was ill. When he was getting better, I offered the barman a drink. We were by ourselves.

"Do you mind if I keep the money instead?" he asked.

"Certainly not. Why ask?"

He proceeded to tell me that before the fruit machines were installed a year earlier, the guests always gave the odd rupee to the staff, but now gave fewer tips as they put them in the one-armed bandits instead. He was buying his house and every rupee counted to him, but half of the staff blew all their wages on the fruit machines, and owed the hotel money, having borrowed to play them. Each night at midnight security guards with alsation guard dogs appeared with trolleys and carted the money away from the machines, and I thought what a menace the fruit machines were to society.

We had a Swedish television crew staying at the hotel. I don't remember seeing them sober, but they were great fun to be with. Our first conversation with them was brief, but funny. Returning at midnight to our bedroom, I heard a crash as I turned the knob of the bathroom door and it refused to budge.

"There must be someone in there", I said.

The friends who slept next door but one came in, rattled the door, and demanded that whoever was in there came out. The friend said "He's afraid to come out," and his wife said "Let's go to the reception desk".

We ran all the way, and breathlessly said, "There's a strange man locked in the bathroom." Dead silence. The clerk, manager and security guards didn't move.

"Quick! Quick! We can't get into our bathroom. There's a man locked in the bathroom," I said, and suddenly the whole lot raced off with what was left of the guests tearing after them. As we turned, four very drunken Swedes were rolling their heads, and said to us, "What is this man locked in? I don't understand. What is this locked in"?

As we got back, we heard various remarks from the people returning to the reception area. "Silly woman. Her husband was in the toilet." "She must have been drunk". "Stupid woman, all that fuss for nothing". The manager explained that the man next door had slipped and fallen, but, although he didn't hurt himself, the vibration caused the bolt to slip in our bathroom, and that it had now been put right.

Jim ordered the heart of the hundred-year-old palm tree as a birthday treat. This is a Mauritian delicacy. After the main course was served I protested that I didn't think I could eat a sweet, when, to my surprise, a magnificent iced birthday cake appeared complete with candles. Tilly, it was packed with ice cream — and mouthwatering. Did I feel spoilt!

The Indian driver said that before they got independence all was peace, but that now there was much corruption and disruptive, political agitators causing trouble, and pointed out huge slogans daubed on the walls round Curepipe and Port Louis — "Black Power".

One evening we recalled his words as we sat out in the moonlight and listened to an Indian, who owned a sizeable slice of the island, negotiating with two white men to build hotels on it, and to import staff to run them. We didn't have any complaints about the staff at the hotel, where all were local people, except for maybe the chef, and visualised a very much changed Mauritius in years to come. We returned home from this piece of paradise, a description of which may seem lengthy to you, but to me, brief. I have not done it justice, and will always remember the warmth and tenderness of the indigenous population.

Two highlights of the journey were on the flight there, being able to recognise fires in the jungle below us and, on the way back, watching the sun rise high above the earth lighting up the silvery streak of the Nile on its journey through the desert.

The guests and staff were delighted to see us back — but, sadly, I regret to say, came the disillusionment, and the end of what we'd believed to be a happy friendship. Hilda had allowed her teenagers to bring in crowds of 18 to 20-year-old yobos, who'd rampaged through the attic and the office, which had always been kept locked unless we were inside, and which they'd been warned to keep locked. In the lounge they had broken silver ornaments which Jim had to get repaired; and they'd taken several books.

The staff complained that each Saturday at five o'clock they'd been ordered to prepare a meal for all of these yobos. The guests complained about the noise and antics, and an old lady lay dying upstairs who had fallen in the night. Hilda was called up by another guest who had heard the fall. They put her to bed, and left her black and blue, placing a note on the kitchen table telling Mai to attened to her. At 10.30 am, when Hilda came down, she called the district nurse, who was horrified and called the doctor. A week later I felt so depressed. Then I thought, "No, I'd rather trust and be caught than waste the precious hours God has given me with suspicion, greed and other horrible thoughts."

If we win the pools, and Mrs Neal is free, we'll all go to Mauritius — even the fit guests would come with us!

Much love,
Lillian.

Tilly my dear,

What an eye-opener it has been attending the local authority conferences, but, first of all, I was glad you all had such a nice holiday and that Sweetpea is doing so well at school. When I was asked if I would like to attend the local authority conferences I thought I would refuse. We thought about it, and said I ought to go to find out what it was all about.

There were 20 local authority wardens and matrons, plus matrons from Dr Barnados homes, Cheshire homes, and Salvation Army homes. We listened to talks by local authority officials, lawyers and social workers, on one day a week, both morning and afternoon. I was the only owner of a private home who had accepted the invitation.

I was surprised to learn that Harold Wilson had enacted legislation for the first time, in 1968, to enable the local authorities to accept people who had money and that nobody can be accepted in a home unless they sign a form giving the local authority control over their money until they die. What is left after they die would naturally go to anybody they had willed it to. They can charge them the full economic rent, but must not touch any capital below £1,000, I thought they said. But another warden said, "I believe it is £2,000. If it isn't now, it soon will be."

It was pointed out, fairly, that in some cases relatives don't want their old people, only the money, but I thought when old people's homes were built the purpose was to look after the people who hadn't any money or relatives, and I wondered what the situation would be if they had 6 vacancies and 12 possible residents on their waiting list. Would not the worst in human nature assert itself by accepting the six rich people, leaving the poor to fend for themselves?

It was planned that when the Labour party got in with a good majority everyone would be taken care of, as they could build warden-based flats throughout the country. Those who couldn't manage to clean their room or cook a breakfast would be moved to Part III accommodation, which means a geriatric ward. Tilly, can you imagine being mentally fit and stuck in a geriatric ward for years? How inhuman!

One official produced a good neighbour scheme, whereby a woman would be paid 10 shillings for each house on her list. She would be responsible for the shopping and make them a cup of tea.

We were told that nobody would ever again be allowed to open a private home for either children or old people.

"How do you propose to stop this?" I asked.

"We will let people who have proved to have a good reputation continue, but will not allow a registration for anyone else."

"But if a person buys a business, and the fire precautions have been passed, how are you going to stop him continuing in a business?"

"It will be the law that every home must have asbestos walls, ceilings and floors. The cost will be too prohibitive."

The lawyer spoke of all the problems the local authority faced when actions were attempted by relatives of residents when there had been a fight or fall among the residents, and of the disputes between staff, wardens and matrons.

One warden stood up and told the story of a nurse coming on night duty an hour late. His wife, a qualified nurse, had administered the drugs. The nurse told her that she shouldn't have done so because she knew she would come in, even if late. An argument developed. The nurse pushed the wife out of the way and a fight broke out. They sacked her, but she won the job back through the tribunal. I was shocked by the whole story. I do not know the rights and wrongs because I wasn't a witness, but common sense would have made me give the nurse a job in another home if I thought she was innocent. What sort of atmosphere could there possibly be to work under in those conditions?

The matrons of the charity homes sat looking glum without speaking a word each week. The lecturer on social work said that their aim was not to have one social worker visit Grandma, another the erring child or another the incompetent mother, but to have one social worker per family. Their duty would be to listen, and try and get the family to relate to each other as opposed to giving advice!

During the lunch breaks several of the wardens talked to me about the running of a private home. They expressed a desire to run one of their own, because, as they put it, "I wouldn't get the same problems, as the people wouldn't be so much trouble because they would be educated." I soon enlightened them that the only difference between people was whether they had courtesy and good manners. Naturally, one might find a higher proportion of courteous and well-mannered people among the educated, but they were quite wrong in thinking that they were all people with integrity. The truth is that human beings are either good, bad, or indifferent throughout society. Most of my guests, fortunately, were delightful, as they were in local authority homes, but both get their share of residents with unacceptable traits.

The wardens complained of red tape and that, given a certain sum of money to spend on improvements in one year, it must be spent or they wouldn't have the same sum next year. And one told me he had ensured it was spent this year by buying stainless steel cutlery, pots, teapots and jugs.

I gave them an account of the expenses of running a private home — the cost of the roof, rates, electricity, oil, laundry, wages, replacements, gardening, food, toiletry, etc — and the need to be ready to get up in the middle of the night, and to nurse, cook, decorate, change fuses, and 101 other things they hadn't thought of. Of how they were protected by the red tape they resented. By the time I'd finished going to the conferences they were far more contented with their jobs.

The residents of a private home can give notice if they're not happy, that is if they are fit enough to look around for another one, so I agree that it is absolutely necessary that homes should be inspected.

I was asked if I would take a social worker full-time on the premises as they said at some time in the future they were going to insist that every home had a social worker.

"What for?" I asked.

"To be a liaison officer between you and your guests," the official replied. Good God Tilly. If I paid a matron there wouldn't be a half-penny to pay the taxman, never mind a social worker. Fancy that, one person to visit 20 people every day and ask them if they have any complaints? You know human nature, some people are always happy and some you can never satisfy. We have noticed if a new guest keeps coming to the office to ask for things to be changed. She keeps on coming no matter how much you attempt to please her.

Ella Wheeler Wilcox got it right when she said that for every lifter there are 20 leaners, so I told them that as far as we were concerned the way we run our home, allowing complete freedom to have visitors from 7 am until midnight, was the only way to ensure that people really had nothing to complain of. When families and friends can pop in and out even at mealtimes and see their meals, and join in the atmosphere, there is no need to pay someone to listen to complaints. There will always be some who complain that it is cold in a heatwave, or it is too hot when there's three feet of snow outside; or they tell a friend who visits every week that they haven't seen you all the week, because they have forgotten they saw you each morning, and kissed you "goodnight" each night.

Heaven forbid that we ever get the sort of world that they visualised at these conferences! What we want is more love towards each other. To quote Kierkegaard: "Everyone in whom the animal disposition is preponderant believes firmly that millions are more than one, whereas spirit is just the opposite, that one is more than millions, and that every man can be that one".

Love is seeing Jesus in each guest and in each member of a caring staff. Love is accepting responsibility. Love is in caring. Love is in respecting an old person's dignity, even when they are irritable or irrational. Love is never asking anyone to do anything you would be ashamed to do yourself. Love is being ready to reassure people with a smile when you clean them up after an accident.

Now, Tilly, think of all the millions of loving people there are in this world, and they know the richness of life that all the planners and talkers would eliminate if they could.

Oh well, Tilly, it was a revelation to us to see how far we have advanced towards that Great Egalitarian Society which is pure myth, but things haven't always worked out as people plan, so having put you in the picture, once again I must say "goodnight" — but not without a smile. Last night our beloved spaniel, Sylvy, slurped down two delicious pieces of golden buttered haddock after I had put a tray on the floor while getting another small table to put in front of me.

Much love,
Lillian.

3rd JANUARY, 1972

Dear Tilly,

Thank you for the flowers and get well messages. It will have been a Christmas we won't forget. Fortunately all preparations were finished before I was forced to stay in bed.

It began with a dear guest, Mrs Murray, spilling her coffee on her breast in the lounge after lunch. She protested that it hadn't burnt her, but we're well aware that liquid doesn't have to be boiling to cause a bad burn on an elderly person, so I insisted on changing her and applying burn oil. She had a very pale pink scar as a result. The following day I checked, and the skin had broken, so I phoned the doctor. He prescribed treatment for her, but, after a week, shingles had developed as a result of the shock.

I nursed her for three weeks, during which time I used to spoon feed her and she often used to stroke my hair when talking to me, and admire the colour. After I'd got some dinner down her on the Thursday I began to feel ill, so I had a bath and came down in my dressing gown to sit with her at 4 pm. She died 15 minutes later. I felt both grieved and ill and went to bed. I spent Friday and Saturday in bed and then thought I ought to make an effort and get up, so I had a bath and noticed a spot on my face and left the bathroom, then still feeling very ill, changed my mind and got back into bed.

Jim entered the room. I said, "I think my blood must be out of order, and that's what's making me feel ill. Look, I've got a spot on my face."

Tilly, you should have seen *his* face. He was staring at me in astonishment.

"One spot! How long since you've looked in the mirror?"

"Five minutes ago," I told him. He handed me a mirror. Ugh! I hadn't noticed that my hands, feet, arms, chest, back, tummy and face were smothered. You never saw such a sight in your life.

Jim phoned the doctor, who, taking one look at me, said, "You poor thing," and that I was proof you can catch chicken pox from shingles.

The staff couldn't remember whether they'd had chicken pox or not, but after listening to Anne's description of me, told Jim that they wouldn't wait on me in case they got chicken pox.

The relatives of guests and friends were marvellous. They helped Jim entertain the guests with the parties, and the outdoor staff popped in for an extra couple of hours throughout Christmas to help the indoor staff, and I thought how fortunate we were to have such caring

*I was covered in spots. You never saw
such a sight in your life.*

people around us. I'm now on my feet and don't feel at all redundant, as I had to begin cleaning all the outsides of the downstairs windows which is a day's work!

Having got Anne off to Lourdes last year I'm planning to send her to Rome this year and help her realise another dream.

I had a remarkably funny dream. I was in a cellar having dinner with Lord Longford, who was in fancy dress as a dragon. Malcolm Muggeridge was dressed in armour. He introduced himself as St George, and the good Cardinal Hume was dressed as Basil Brush. Malcolm Muggeridge asked me what I was going to eat and the visor of his helmet kept falling over his mouth. The waiter offered me some gruyere cheese.

"Have some of this. The more you eat the bigger the holes get, so you get more for your money." he said.

Looking up I saw Dennis Healey with a halo saying to Lord Longford, "You've got to put your money in the bank, Frank." I woke up as Jim was using an old fashioned tin opener to cut the armour that I was wearing, off me.

It was such a colourful dream and obviously the result of something I've read in different papers about them throughout the week, and they have all got mixed up in the one dream. When one has instant recall to such delightful dreams one becomes aware that one lives two lives —one while asleep. Who needs television when one has one's own shows every night?

Jim made me laugh yesterday morning when he told me his dreams. He said he was walking down a quiet country road when a telephone, that was placed in a hedge, began to ring. He picked up the receiver and a voice said "This is Brezhnev calling from Moscow". Jim thought, "Gosh, he wants Lillian."

Birds, scenery, music, politicians, friends, animals, royalty, TV personalities, poets, painters, authors, guests, friends, acquaintances, all crowd my colourful dreams. I've been pursued by Ted Heath throughout a locked House of Commons in term after someone whispered to me, "Haven't you noticed that when he takes a fancy to a woman she's never seen again?". I've argued with Harold Wilson who suggested that we ought to emigrate, and I've told him that he talked sense. I've ordered the two Ronnies to paint a room; little Ronnie standing on big Ronnie's shoulders painting like mad. I could go on and on. There are about 500 a year recorded. If anyone is depressed I choose a diary and we soon find ourselves laughing about some stupid silly situation that can only occur in a dream.

I would like to run an early morning radio programme called "Dream Half Hour" on which we could all enjoy listening to other people's silly dreams, and there would be a record of the precognitive ones.

One of the most humorous dreams was when I tipped a taxi driver £6,200 and he said with astonishment, "This is the biggest tip I've ever had." One week later, Jim woke me and, kneeling beside me, handed me a letter saying, "For you, O Queen of the Pooliverse." It was a cheque for £6,250. As you can see even in dreams what you give comes back!

Mother always used to say, when I was young, never refuse anybody anything, whether it's food or money if you have it, and never look for it to be rewarded, but God will always see that you have help when you need it. How true that has proved to be!

It's time I put the sweet pea seeds to germinate, or we won't have the garden full of multi-coloured butterfly wings, with enchanting perfume surrounding us.

Yesterday was cook's day off and I discovered she'd got semolina in several tins and tapioca in another two, so I collected three empty seven pound tins, and 20 four-pound tins, went down to the village for an assortment of paints and brushes, and more than half the guests helped paint them. We had great fun. Now we have a blue tin with a ship painted in white, *S/S Semolina*, and every tin is a different colour with contrasting paints describing the contents in a humorous fashion. You should see the brightly coloured tins on their shelves. They look most attractive. I'd better think of more things to paint so we can have more entertaining afternoons!

Time to say "goodnight."

I'll phone on Sunday.

Much love,
Lillian.

3rd APRIL, 1972

My dear Tilly,

Thank you for a lovely long letter. It was highly amusing and just what we needed. Jim had a shock! Old Ma Gilbert wrote to say she would come to lunch to discuss the lease. She hasn't set her foot inside the place for 13 years! She arrived and praised everything she saw.

"Marvellous. It really looks most attractive," she said, and she continued on in this way until we sat down to lunch. Jim asked if she'd sell the freehold. She refused, so he asked for a 21 year lease. She disagreed, but agreed to a 17 year lease. She questioned us about staff, food, the intercom, the gardeners and so on, and, on leaving, said she would phone.

The following week she phoned and said in view of fixing the new rent, she'd like to bring her surveyor over. We should have smelt a rat, but we didn't. She arrived with three men, one of whom was her surveyor. We offered them coffee and then left them in the lounge, telling them that we would come back when we had attended to some urgent tasks. They wandered round inside and out, inspecting the building and leaving shortly before lunch.

One week later we got a letter from her telling us that she was coming back and taking the place over! Jim's cousin who had been his solicitor died two years ago. When he'd bought the business and protested that the lease should be for 21 years Mrs Gilbert had said to them, "I'll be an old woman by then. I should never want it back. I'll keep on renewing it for you." His cousin was old and obviously past it. However, when he died, Jim rang his accountant, who brought his solicitor to dinner. This new solicitor assured us that she would have to renew the lease, and that we hadn't any problems. Jim immediately rang this new solicitor.

"Oh she can do that, but she must pay you a thousand pounds compensation."

"You swore she never could," said Jim angrily, and continued to say that we would fight it in the courts.

We phoned our barrister friend and made arrangements to see Counsel for advice. The next day we had an unexpected visit from a friend at court who told us that he'd just handled the application from Mrs Gilbert to change the house into luxury flats for old people, as it had an intercom system and full fire precautions installed. Armed with this knowledge we went to see a freshly chosen solicitor who had been over the day before to discuss the problem.

142

Three days after this we went to London to see a barrister. I grew angrier and angrier as he swivelled in his chair.

"It's a lovely looking house," he said, as he gazed at the photograph. "She is the owner, and the judge will say to himself, "Does she look responsible? Is she capable?""

"But she is 74!" I exploded.

"Exactly, and the judge might be 74. If he says she's too old, he says he's too old."

Eventually, I got mad. I said, "Look, she paid £6,000 for it, and within three years the local authorities ordered her to close it. She sold the furniture for £3,000 and the business for £2,000 to him. He had to put in all the fire escapes and fire precautions that she refused to do. He has put in oil-fired central heating, an intercom system and kept it in tip top repair inside and out. In some countries people get shot for less than that."

"You say the local authorities were going to close her down. Have you proof?"

"We can't find the papers. We know Jim found them when he moved in. The local authorities have said that they would come to court to prove us to have a good reputation. They've told us so."

"Exactly, but they won't say that the other lady defaulted, and you've no proof."

We argued on and on. Eventually we shook hands, and he said he would do all he could to help us.

We thought that it could cost us a bomb, and reflected that we might go bankrupt, as we were told it would cost between £60,000 and £100,000 if the judge were to say we must pay the costs, and we hadn't got half of £60,000.

"You might win and have to pay the costs, or lose and have to pay them. However, if you lose you'll come out covered in glory," said Counsel. That wasn't what I wanted at all, just satisfaction. If there was any justice, the local authority knew the truth and they should have made a compulsory purchase of the house, and made sure the old people would always have a home.

We returned home very down in the mouth, and discussed the problem until the early hours of the morning.

"I am not giving these people notice whatever happens. We'll look for another house where we can take the lot, or buy a business where there is room to re-accommodate them. I'm sure any local authority would be reasonable, when our local authority confirms the predicament we were placed in," I said.

Jim said, "House and business prices are rising. You are going to find it difficult to find anything that would suit us and the guests at a price we can afford, and I'd never touch another leasehold house after this."

The next day I phoned the agents for rest and nursing homes, and made arrangements with the taxi driver to take me to the south coast. One of the owners had invited me to stay the night, as he had said I might like to look round the area. I phoned the owner of a large country home who wanted to lease half of it. In spite of what Jim said I didn't think we should leave one stone unturned in our search for a new home and, anyway, it was going to be a costly journey, so I thought as it was en route there would be nothing lost.

We set off at 5 am, as we were going to Somerset, Cornwall, Dorset and Sussex. Miss Brain, the taxi-driver, is always taking either me or one of the guests out, so she knows us well, and I told her of our predicament on the journey. We arrived at the stately home by 9.30 am. Tilly, was it "stately"! You could have put this house in the kitchen and it would have been lost. It seemed nearly the size of Blenheim Palace.

The owner, a man in his 40s, offered us a sherry in the library and then gave us a conducted tour of part of the house. Oil paintings filled the great hall and looked down from the galleries. Tilly, it was magnificent, and an extension to the main building contained 15 beautifully furnished bedrooms, with lounges, kitchen and library furnished equally expensively below. Eventually the owner asked me to take it over plus the flat, of which the furnishings were to be purchased. A wealthy oil company director had terminated his lease on it and moved. He then mooted the problem of the insurance on the oil paintings, as having visitors, I would have to be responsible for this. Apparently the director had always helped when there was a crisis on the farm, especially during harvesting, and the owner presumed we would do the same. As he was retired I'm not surprised he moved. I said I doubted that my husband would agree. He said he hoped he would, and, promising to phone, we parted amicably.

He'd insisted that we ate before we moved on, so we were able to quickly inspect another six places as we motored round to Sussex, where we arrived at 9 pm. Four of the six were in built-up areas, and of these only one was well run, with the same owners for 25 years. Of the two that were in the country, one was a write-off. I saw that they owed vast bank charges, plus a mortgage. The other people wanted a terrific price, but it was genuine. They offered a lease, but I refused.

Eventually we arrived at the home where we'd been offered a room for the night. Tilly, my heart sank to my shoes, as did Miss Brain's. On the phone he'd described it as facing a parkland and a hundred yards off the sea. The parkland had been built all round at about the turn of the century, and the next morning I walked through four streets and

144

crossed a main road before I glimpsed the sea! They did everything they could to make us welcome. A small sitting room had a dozen people sitting around the walls watching a TV, and they kept telling us how the relatives always gave them large sums of money for Christmas in gratitude for looking after the relatives (something that's never happened to us in 14 years).

"Why are you selling?" I asked.

"I want to run a greengrocers," he said.

"Would you mind giving me the accounts now? I'll study them when I get to bed." And study them I did, with Miss Brain who is well used to accounts, as she owns a large garage.

He had terrific mortgage repayments which he hadn't kept up, only the interest, and had large bank loans unpaid. I pointed to the doors that had pieces of asbestos nailed on them leaving a three inch gap between the edge of the door all round.

"The Fire Department never passed that. He's up to his ears in trouble, Miss Brain. What a shock!" She agreed, and we slept fitfully that night.

I rose at 5.45 am. After I'd dressed I walked through the streets to buy a newspaper, and found out how far away the sea was, as I've already told you. When I returned I went into the kitchen with Miss Brain, where we were offered breakfast. We refused, but accepted a cup of tea.

Miss Brain, looking round the kitchen, noted 12 trays with tea pots, milk, sugar and half a piece of white sliced bread and butter on each plate.

"Are they having a cooked breakfast or just cereals and an egg?" asked Miss Brain.

"Oh no. They wouldn't eat breakfasts like that. They don't need much food. It's money for nothing. It would all come back and be thrown out if we gave them breakfasts like that," he announced airily.

Miss Brain said "Where did you get the idea that you could run an old people's home?"

"Oh, the wife worked in one and could see it was money for nothing."

Miss Brain told him that she often saw our guests eating a variety of cereals, toast, eggs, and a couple had bacon and eggs and that the sooner they gave up looking after old people the better it would be for the old people who lived there. We left immediately and stopped to call at five more places on the way back again. Only one was seemingly well-run, and again the people had been running it for years and didn't owe money. Of the other four, the guests seemed happy enough in three of them, but the accounts told me that all was not well.

In the last place we visited I really felt sorry for the woman. She had six guests, very disabled, in a dark lounge. The house was magnificent, but needed a fortune spent on it, and the acre of ground hadn't had a mower over it in years. She explained that she only had one helper and she was away for the day. I studied the accounts. They had run the business for 10 years.

"You owe a lot of money," I said.

"Oh, I don't understand accounts," said the affable, good-looking husband.

I said I was in a hurry and would phone when I got back. I felt so sorry for the wife who I felt was conscientious and harassed. Dark circles of worry surrounded her eyes. She was well-educated and kind I thought, so when we arrived back I phoned her and said we wouldn't buy, but I hoped she'd sell soon because I could see she needed a rest.

"Would you like to make us some kind of offer?" she said. I told her I was sorry that we couldn't afford to spend the money on the place that I could see needed spending, and asked her what her husband did for a living.

"He's an accountant!" she replied.

We settled with Miss Brain and I could have wept. We argued with her, but she was adamant that Jim should check the mileage and only pay for that. She said that what she'd seen and heard in 48 hours had opened her eyes.

We talked for three hours although I was exhausted. I described each place and discussed what I'd seen and what I had not seen, and of the reasons given for selling not being the true reasons in many cases. Most people buy such businesses in ignorance or, in some cases, because of idealism, and then find the snags, which, either by lack of experience or by temperament, they are unable to cope with.

As you will have observed, the man who put us up for the night was stupid, ignorant and should never have been allowed to get a registration for his home, but his conversation with a local authority official would have been quite different. He would have been whining and telling him he gave them fillet steak, I shouldn't be surprised.

You will remember the saga of the local authority conferences I attended, and of how most of the wardens and matrons had wanted to run their own private home, until they had talked to me about the expenses and problems. People can always spend other people's money, but they don't like spending their own, and as there are many good people who run both local authority and private homes, so there are as many we could wish to have a more Christian and loving attitude towards people.

146

We've decided to look for a house in case we lose our battle, so that we can take the people with us.

Will phone soon.

Thanks for all your news.

Love,
Lillian.

Tilly dear,

You remarked in your last letter about the lack of discipline and respect in children today, and, although I agree with you, fortunately there are still some responsible people who bring up their children well, but what headaches they must face and worries about what the children see when in school, where they mix with children not so fortunate as themselves.

Funny you should write about that, because the next day Mrs Hart had a visit from her granddaughter with her husband and four children — of six, four, three and two years of age. All hell was let loose here, and the old lady's delight in looking forward to seeing them was ruined by the most outrageous tantrums, especially from the four-year-old girl and three-year-old boy.

The mother sacked the nanny last week because she refused to indulge the children in their choice of what they would like to eat at breakfast. Their mother told us that a child should be indulged and that they would mature more quickly and soon lose any destructive traits they possessed! It was as if a hurricane had hit the old lady's room. The children pulled open drawers, scattered things around, broke the switch on the radio and attempted to use the talking book machine, but I'd gone in on hearing the commotion and rescued it. The three-year-old boy threw himself flat on the floor in the corridor and screamed with rage.

"Don't take any notice of him. He'll stop when he finds nobody takes any notice of him," said the mother. The six-year-old boy and four-year-old girl rushed into the hall and, pushing the top off the two fish tanks, began splashing the water around in haste to catch one of the fish!

Jim came through with his face red, ordered them away, and put the top back, while I cleared up the water. The three-year-old was still shrieking and the father went back, picked him up and carried him screaming through the hall out to the car where they all got in and drove back home.

What a relief and what a ghastly lot they will turn out to be! Mrs Hart was terribly upset, not because of what they had done to her room, but because of the attitude of her granddaughter and, as she said, she hadn't any consideration for any guest in the house.

It's always a delight when relatives bring children into the house, and they are always made a great fuss of by other guests. This time was the exception. There was a great sigh of relief at their departure! Jim said he would have smacked their bottoms as he'd had his smacked a couple of times before he was six years old, and its rare that you have to smack a child after that.

Sometimes Tilly, you see a guest behaving badly and you know it is because he or she didn't get a smacked bottom when very young. Lady Dance is a perfect example. Her son told us that his mother has never let anyone oppose her in life, that his grandmother had said she always got her own way — and now she's impossible, Tilly.

We have told the guests' relatives in the hope that everything will turn out all right and that we'll win. Then they won't have been worried for nothing.

Mrs Scott, who has been with us five years, and had attempted suicide a month before she came to us because she was told that she only had a couple of months to live, is very fond of us and very happy. She came into the office a fortnight ago and said that Lady Dance had approached her with a petition and asked her to sign it. It was to ask the owner of the property if she could ensure that all the guests would receive the same care and freedom that they had now, and that any changes would be only for the guests' benefit.

I was furious that the son or daughter of one of the guests must have broken their word, so the following Sunday we spoke privately to Lady Dance's son and told him he must stop his mother sending the letter. He said it would be very difficult as his mother always overruled everyone.

However, he promised he would try and reason with her. Before he left he said he'd had his mother's word that she wouldn't send the letter.

Last Wednesday, Lady Dance was out as usual. Everyone knows that she's away all day on Wednesday. I could hear her phone ringing. At first I took no notice, but I thought it might be someone who was unaware that she was out and had got an urgent message.

I went to her room, picked up the phone and heard Mrs Gilbert's voice. She said, "Lady Dance?"

"Yes," I said as deeply as I could.

"Oh good, I want to reassure you that I will look after every guest as if I were their own mother. There won't be any changes. That is Lady Dance isn't it?"

"Yes," I replied.

"Now you most reassure them all that I will love them very much."

"Yes, Yes." It was so unexpected I was trembling.

"Pass my message round won't you, and thank you for writing to me."

"Yes, good morning," I said, and hung up.

149

I rushed down to Jim. "What a pair of blasted liars. They deserve each other. If she comes back could you imagine Ma Gilbert's face when Lady Dance thunders, "Madam, you never replied to my letter!"?

I've never forgotten when she had all the furniture changed round while I was on holiday and I had it all put back.

"Madam, how dare you!" she thundered. So you now have some idea of the type of personality she is. There is one consolation; if we leave we'll be leaving Lady Dance behind.

You asked me about diets. We only have one diabetic, which doesn't present any problems, but we managed to employ extra help while we went to London to see the solicitor. We arrived back at 4 pm. Jim went to prepare the food for the chickens and found broad beans in the chicken bowl.

"What's this, Mai?" he asked. It turned out that Anne had given Jenny five tins of broad beans instead of gooseberries, and they were served as sweet with custard. Mai said only six plates came back untouched!

Could you believe it? The guests laughed when I apologised and they said, "You've got so much to do, don't worry about it."

Since decimalisation the prices here have shot up, and I've been reading for years that inflation is unavoidable. At the moment we burn 60 gallons of oil a day. Supposing oil should reach £1 a gallon, then the total income we get for a week would not be sufficient to pay the oil bill.

In one sense the place is elegant and spacious. Jim has made it look elegant, or should I say added to the original elegance, but I realise it is quite uneconomical to run. The Doctor said to me more than once, "You've never charged enough." It should have been a nursing home because there would have been six very spacious wards apart from the private rooms.

If we fail to win over the lease then we will take consolation from the fact that we won't have to face the enormous heating, electricity and maintenance bills that we could be faced with if inflation increases. The pensions would probably rise with the inflation and I can foresee that all sorts of changes would have to be made to stay in business — such as sharing bedrooms. This is necessary where people need attention during the night, but it is not an ideal arrangement where people have retained their mental faculties. Privacy is essential to enable a person to retain dignity.

Oh, Tilly, words could never express the joy of loving and being loved! I wish that everyone shared this joy. There wouldn't be anyone living alone and neglected if we all felt this tremendous love for our fellow human beings. People talk of happiness, but most people don't realise that to strive for happiness is stupid. It's usually a world of fantasy where they see themselves as another type of human being — the film star, pop star, president, prime minister or royalty; rich, powerful and being worshipped. True happiness is doing and giving, in being wanted, in sharing and in recognising that the same young person is in the ageing body.

William Blake was so right when he wrote:

Man was made for Joy and Woe
And when this we rightly know,
Through the world we safely go,
Joy and Woe are woven fine,
A clothing for the soul divine.

Blake may have been poor in material things, but how rich he was spiritually! And he wasn't a prude either.

Well, Tilly, I must get on with the next job, and we have John and Alison coming to dinner tonight.

Look forward to your news.

> Much love,
> Lillian.

Dear Tilly,

Your remark about Mr Shalk, reminded me that there was a lot I didn't tell you after I came back from Mauritius to face the chaos which Hilda had caused. Mr Shalk died a few weeks before we went to Mauritius.

He was heard walking down the corridor at 3 am and one of the guests called me on the intercom to tell me that there was someone about. I investigated and found all the lights on downstairs and discovered Mr Shalk in the dining room. He said he was waiting for his lunch. I persuaded him to go back to bed but the following night I left the intercom box in his room switched on so that I could hear him if he moved — which he did — once again going down to the dining room at 2 am.

The following day he walked downstairs holding his trousers up instead of wearing a belt. He argued that he'd never worn a belt which was nonsense. I called the doctor in and he confirmed that it would only be a matter of weeks before he died.

I rang his son Hans and explained the situation. He said he would come in and help me everyday if his father could die in peace with us, to which I readily agreed. He quickly deteriorated after many arguments with cheerful, jolly Hans about the way he should dress. The last two weeks I nursed him in bed and, putting his dinner through the blender, I spoon-fed him.

Hans would spend the evening with him and I would get up if I heard a movement on the intercom.

During the last week Hans said, "My wife and I have been talking for the last two years about our retirement which isn't far off, and we'd decided to buy an old people's home because one would be sure of making good money. Now I've seen just what you have to put up with and I've changed my mind. You earn every penny you get."

I invited him down to the office and showed him the books. He was astonished. "Good God! You don't earn a quarter of my income. I wouldn't dream of working like you and taking all the responsibilities you do for that sum," said Hans.

"Well, some people make more; some people less. It depends on whether one's mean or charging very high fees. Most important is the happiness of all concerned," I told him.

The day after Mr Shalk died we had to go to London to have injections and left Hilda in charge. When we returned Anne said, "Mrs Jarvis (Hilda) couldn't find the orange juice. I searched everywhere."

"What did she want the orange juice for, Anne?" I asked.

"Mr Shalk's son — not Mr Hans — the other brother. He came at 9 am and after he'd registered his father's death he was back at 10.30 am. He had drinks with Mrs Jarvis and lunch. Then they had drinks until four o'clock," said Anne.

Tilly, my heart sank. Jim and I have never touched a drink in the daytime except one on anniversaries. Jim said "We'll cancel the holiday."

"But we've paid the money. Now we'll have to take as many precautions as we can to ensure that the place is run properly," I said.

After Mr Shalk's cremation, Han's brother brought four pot plants. He said, "Would you give them to Rose, May and Jenny and this one to Mrs Jarvis who did so much for my father?"

I was speechless. She'd never been near him or did a thing for him. We felt less and less like taking a holiday, but it was too late to find anyone else to take over.

We emphasised that the office was always kept locked when we weren't inside. On the top shelf on one side of the office was nearly a hundred pounds' worth of cigarettes. We left them a sum of cash in case of emergency and we left a £100 with the neighbours so that we didn't have to rush to the bank on our return.

On the day we returned, we collected the cash and locked it in the office drawer and Jim went to sleep for a couple of hours while I rushed off to get another pair of spectacles made up. Jim had broken my others by sitting on them, the day we flew back. When I returned Jim asked me if I had taken cash to the optician. I said, "No. The cheque book." "Well, there's £20 missing from the drawer," he said. Then I looked up and noticed there wasn't one cigarette left. I'd written to you about the silver being smashed and the wild parties held by hippies while we were away. We were in the dumps as we thought what fools we'd been to trust this very attractive woman.

Later while inspecting the gun room which had been made ready for a new guest, Mrs Smythe Robinson wandered in and sat in a chair smoking. "You're always busy, lamb," she said.

"Not always, but often," I replied. There was a silence for a few minutes, then I heard, "I wouldn't give my money to that Mrs Jarvis. I could see she wasn't a worker."

"What do you mean Mrs Smythe Robinson?"

"She said, 'I'll sell my house and you give me your money, then I'll buy an old people's home, or a big house like this and we'll run it in partnership. You'll always be looked after, and all the guests here would prefer to come with me than stay with Mrs Mannooch'."

Tilly, I was staggered. This reminded me of Mrs Davies whom I consoled every day for two years. One evening a week she went to the WI and became friendly with a fifty-year-old widow who offered her accommodation with her. She told her that she was too young at 60 years of age to be in an old peoples' home.

Mrs Davies's son agreed to the move but he wasn't very happy five weeks later when his mother was unceremoniously dumped outside the village hairdresser's with her suitcases. "You dirty creature. Don't you dare come to my house again," said the widow to a wildly sobbing Mrs Davies. It turned out that she'd surprised Mrs Davies trying to get into bed with her 20-year-old son.

Almost a year after this the same widow took another 60-year-old guest who'd been with us twelve months and again put her out on the street within a fortnight. We had a frantic call from the son asking us to take her back but the room had been let. This widow, a Mrs Brookes, had never got on with anyone. She'd fallen out with neighbours in each of the luxury flats her son had arranged for her. She spent her life interfering and trying to improve everyone! While with us she bought a bed tray and then tried to persuade every guest to buy one. "Instead of balancing a tray on your lap its on a stand on wheels and can be pushed away from the bed," she explained. One gentlemen only was persuaded — the padre. Within a week he was most distressed, due to the fact that he'd fallen asleep, turned over, and the tray load of china was smashed to pieces. He said it couldn't happen when you had a simple tray, because you placed it on the bedside chair if you wanted to go back to sleep.

Within the month Mrs Brookes did exactly the same thing. She rushed to us and apologised. The widow-woman that Mrs Brookes went to, soon found out that everything she cooked had been put on too early or too late!

You know, I think our hair would stand on end if we knew of some of the stories that owners and matrons could tell of the residents in both private and local authority homes. It is an absolute necessity that inspection and checks are made on both, but in our experience the idea that a social worker should go round seeking complaints is quite ludicrous. People will always complain, and in some cases the less they have to complain about the more they will complain.

Last night we were talking about the last general election which we discussed at some length. All the guests have postal votes and we go to each guest while they are all together in the lounge and tell them to put their cross against the Party they wish to support. Last time three of the guests' relatives, two Conservative and one Labour, said to Jim, "Half of these people don't know what they're voting for, so you can get their signature and put the cross in for them." Jim was indignant and told them off, but last night we discussed this matter and wondered if this was done in other homes, and if so whether it balanced out. If twenty homes did this to influence people to vote Conservative might not it also work out that twenty homes would use their influence to support Labour?

I thought that the representatives from each party should visit together all old people's homes to ensure that the people were not influenced.

One of our guests said to me, "I don't think any old person should have a vote unless he's mentally fit." I reminded him that many young people have the vote who are not mentally fit and that many people of all ages who vote, haven't a clue as to the problems that face politicians. They themselves get a shock when they achieve power.

Yesterday Mr Jarvis celebrated his 90th birthday, I gave him a kiss on his cheek as I wished him many happy returns. As I walked off he said, "Just a minute, I'm 90 today, not 1!"

A very beautiful 65-year-old widow arrived to begin a new life with us in Mr Shalk's room. She must have been stunning when young. However, it was unfortunate that we had to get her moved into a nursing home within a week. She kept wandering into our lounge picking up books and other objects and taking them into the office to Jim. She never spoke, just stood there with a beaming smile on her face. After a few days of this behaviour, which puzzled us, we were astonished to discover that she had visited each male guests' bedroom in a see through nightdress in the middle of the night. The padre, the doctor and the other male guests reported her to us, but all expressed sympathy for her except Mr Jarvis who said, "I wouldn't mind a young woman, but I don't want a bloody old woman like that in my room!"

Everything seems to happen in threes. The next guest to take Mr Shalk's room had a heart attack within a week. She was followed by a Mrs Potter. The name Potty would have been more apt. We'd had a call from both the local authorities. Apparently she had been found on the floor of her bungalow and there wasn't any accommodation they could place her in for another five days, so I agreed to take her for five days.

I was surprised to find a well made up woman who appeared to be in her early forties. Actually she was 50. We showed her to her room. When I returned to show her around she was stark naked on the floor. "Not again, not another one," I thought. Oh dear Tilly, I really wished those 5 days to speed by. The only time she was dressed was in bed. She spent hours putting on the lipstick and mascara, and we nearly strangled ourselves trying to lift her off the floor on to the bed.

The night before they took her away I said, "I'll pop up and make sure she's in bed." Ahead of me was our handsome genial 92-year-old Dr King. Having arrived on the landing he bent at the knees and holding the left knee with the left hand moved his glasses forward to the tip of his nose to intently study the nether regions of the prone and naked lady.

We struggled to get her back to bed but collapsed with laughter at the sight of Dr King making his inspection. The next morning I was on the phone pronto. The local authority man said, "Now you know why her husband was glad to leave this world. He put up with that for 15 years. She has a daughter who refuses to have anything to do with her." When the ambulance men arrived they groaned, "Not her again." One said they'd taken her to mental hospitals so many times that they'd nearly developed hernias from lifting her off the floor.

Mrs Haines and Mrs Hart have both died. Mrs Hart had been here 10 years and we do miss this courageous lively character very much. Two weeks before she died we felt depressed when Jim said he dreamt that an angel stood on top of the main staircase and said, "I've come for number three." A great gold halo surrounded the angel. Mrs Hart's room was number three and we knew then that she would be leaving us.

Mrs Haines had always had her meals in her room as she was so eccentric but I know you'll enjoy the following story. She had this hatred of electricity and used to wander from one side of the road to the other making signs in front of the telegraph poles. The police discussed the likelihood of her getting knocked down and agreed that if such a thing occurred, no driver would be blamed. We felt that as she'd been locked up for 40 years she should enjoy her freedom. She wore skirts to the ground and a large picture hat. Her voice was delightful and the guests in the adjacent rooms to her, she addressed as Royalty. She told us that she'd have a word with the Queen and had the titles Count and Countess bestowed on us, plus giving us shares in the coal mines!

The doctor was superb when we had to call him out to her. He told her that the Queen had gone on holiday and sent him to examine her. It was the same performance with clothes. We used to tell her that Her Majesty had sent them. When we had a lot of guests down with 'flu one year Jim asked her if she'd help by placing her tray on a table on the landing to save us coming all the way around the landing. "Yes," she said. Two days later he asked her again, as she failed to put it out. "Oh, I can't do that. I had an audience with the Queen who told me not to do it," she replied.

"Well perhaps you'd ask for another audience as so many people are sick with the 'flu that we're being pushed very hard," said Jim.

"No, she doesn't allow a second audience," was the reply.

Each year the Lord Chancellor's visitor visited Mrs Haines to check on her welfare and condition. He would discuss her health and any other problem with us and then talk to her by herself for half an hour.

Before she died, a different Lord Chancellor's visitor stepped out of the chauffeur driven car. We were busy painting, so we only had a few quick words with him before serving tea to him and Mrs Haines in the hall.

As he was leaving he said, "I'm surprised to find such a normal and delightful woman. I was expecting to meet somebody quite different according to the files. The only thing that puzzles me is her hatred of the Poles. Is it because she's lived in Poland some time?" he asked.

We said, "No," and after saying goodbye we looked at each other and then the penny dropped as the car drove out of the gates. It was the poles carrying the electricity cables that she put spells on!

You asked after Dr Scott. She's in a nursing home. Her mental faculties had been deteriorating for years and I'd had to take her to the toilet every couple of hours to prevent her spending a penny on the floor. The toilet was within two feet of her door, yet Rose told me that day after day she caught her sitting in the wash basin with her feet on a chair as she said other people used the toilet and that it was unhygienic to sit on a lavatory seat after other people had used it. I felt sorry for her because she had been a clever doctor according to her niece.

A couple of months before we had her removed we found she was missing. We were beside ourselves with worry as we searched for her. Four hours later I said, "The cornfield. We haven't searched the cornfield."

The corn was almost above my head. However, we began a systematic search and eventually found her inside a huge stack of wood that had been left in the field. She'd climbed it and fell inside. Jim raced back and brought the car to the entrance of the field, then we lifted her out and carried her to the car, then put her to bed once we got back to the house.

We rang the doctor. He arrived, examined her and said that she'd recover the use of her legs, which she did.

When we visited her in the nursing home she said, "Ring the bell for the waiter. You must dine with me!" They were very kind to her there and so we're not worried about her.

Last week I heard cook say to Anne, "There's no need to go to confession this week. We went last week and you've got nothing to confess."

Anne said, "Ah sure and I've got me improper thoughts to confess, so I'll be going now. Look at that cat. Would you say it is a good catholic cat?" said she laughing.

"Don't be silly. Cats aren't catholics," replied cook.

"Sure they are. Did ye not hear the story Father told us about the cat owned by Paddy, who had kittens. He said to the priest, 'Please father. Me wife is driving me mad about getting a home for the kittens. Will ye ask the congregation on Sunday if some good soul will give a home to the kittens?'

'Just a minute, Paddy. What denomination are these kittens?' asked the Priest.

'Catholics, father. Sure good catholics,' answered Paddy. Not one of the congregation offered them a home, so Paddy asked the Anglican Minister who asked him what denomination they were, and he told him Church of England.

Two weeks later Paddy went back to the priest saying, 'Oh, father. Please ask again, for sure. Isn't me wife's bad temper over the kittens making life unbearable for me?'

'Wait Paddy. You said they were Catholics. Then you told the Anglican minister they were Church of England. Why did you lie Paddy?'

'Ah sure, father. Their eyes weren't opened when I told him that'."

The kitchen rang with laughter, which it often does.

Well Tilly, this has been an exceptionally long letter. I noted your last letter to me contained 12 pages. Thank God most of the guests are mentally alert and we have some very interesting conversations. We've found throughout the years that two thirds of the guests have only physical ailments and the other third make the highlights of the letters I write to you.

It reminds me that a man introduced a "good news only" paper in America. He went bust!

Before I go to sleep I must tell you about Mrs Butler. We were asked if we would take her mother for a fortnight by a pleasant Mrs Lewis, who said that the doctor said it was essential for her to get a rest. As we had a vacancy that was to be filled in three weeks time, we agreed.

The following day Mrs Lewis arrived and said to me, "What do I tell mother?"

"What? You mean to say you haven't told her she's coming to us for a fortnight's holiday?" I said.

"No. I didn't know what to say," she replied. I went out and introduced myself to a bright, blue-eyed, round faced Mrs Butler. Taking her into the lounge I introduced her to the other guests and left her sitting there. Mrs Lewis gave me the address of her sister with whom she'd been living.

Oh dear. Every half hour I had to explain that her daughter would be back for her and that she was only on holiday. Sitting in the dining room at 7.15 pm, as everyone was finishing the meal, Mrs Butler began to sing "Around the Marble Arch, round and round we march." By the time they'd all got over the shock, a few joined in with her. They quickly regretted it because she never stopped until I took her to bed at 9.30 pm. I undressed her, tucked her up and bid her goodnight.

Settling down in the lounge at 10 pm I heard, "Cooee, Joan! Cooee Joan." It was Mrs Butler. Every ten minutes I put her back to bed until 11.15 pm, when I gave two Soneryls and waited until she fell asleep.

After five days of "Round the Marble Arch," and following me everywhere, she suddenly decided that the house was hers. "Switch that TV off. I don't want these people in my lounge," she said. I phoned the sister and explained that the guests had never had their peace disturbed by another guest and asked them if they would mind taking her back.

They were here within the hour and thanked us and then told us their story. They were farmers who'd retired and bought a small cottage. Twelve months later the sister became widowed and the mother said she wanted to sell her house and live with the widowed daughter. They decided to sell the cottage and buy a big house so that they could divide it into three flats, and all live together, but lead their own lives. The mother had gone round the bend, the widowed daughter had long bouts of crying, and the married daughter had lost two stone in weight worrying about them both.

I refused to take any money in this case because I'd had to ask them to remove the mother. They were very grateful but, oh Tilly, the mother needed to be under medical supervision and should have been placed in a psychiatric nursing home where there are sufficient staff to cope. The money from the sale of her house would have paid for her keep. Unfortunately some people don't want to part with the money.

Now it's time for bed. Look forward to your news.

Much love,
Lillian.

My dear Tilly,

Your letter couldn't have arrived at a more appropriate time. It was a tonic, as I'd just had a phone call that sent me into the depths of despair. Our great and good friends, Vera and Sylvia, who live in the heart of the stockbroker belt, had inspected a house near to them that we had hoped to buy and take our four guests with us.

It was quite adequate, with six bedrooms and three reception rooms. When they first rang us they said, "It would be lovely to have you near us. There's a house for sale. Shall we inspect it?" We were both over the moon at the prospect of living near to them, but half an hour before your letter arrived they rang and described the house, and then dropped a bombshell.

"You won't be able to bring any guests with you because they're rather snooty, and we've been told that they stopped one lady from taking elderly guests 'in this area'."

What sort of people are they? Certainly not human beings. Where will they go when they're old? Well, these are the facts, Tilly. Now I wouldn't want to live with such people round me. We'll soon find another house, so let me tell you the story I told the guests yesterday afternoon.

In Mount Street, London, there died a man named Martin Van Buckell in 1810. He was quite a character; a quack doctor and a dentist of celebrity. He applied for the post of dentist to George III. When the consent of His Majesty was obtained, he said he did not care for the custom of Royalty. When his wife died he had her body embalmed and kept her in the parlour. His first wife he made to dress in black, and the second wife in white. He allowed his beard to grow, which was considered madness at that time. He sold the hairs from his beard for a guinea each to ladies who wanted to become mothers of fine children! His printed circular described him as a "British Christian man with a comely beard, full eight inches long".

He lived in the same house over 50 years, and patients had to come to him. "I go to none," he said, and kept his word even when offered £500. He painted his house with spots, and he would sit on his doorstep and sell oranges, cakes and gingerbread to the children. He stayed a teetotaller all his life.

The guests were delighted with the bit about selling a hair of his beard for a guinea. The Colonel said he'd stop shaving if he could get a guinea a hair, and the Major said (amid laughter) that the ladies probably got something extra as a kind of guarantee that it worked!

Thank God for eccentrics, but I couldn't have stood being the second wife with the first one in the parlour! By the way, he never spoke to his children. He just whistled them.

This produced a spate of stories. The Colonel said that Sarah, Duchess of Marlborough, pressed her husband to take his medicine in front of the doctor by saying, "I'll be hanged if it does not prove serviceable." Dr Garth then said, "Do take it then my Lord Duke, for it must be of service one way or another."

The Major came back with a story about a man who was given a lift when he and a friend, a police chief, were motoring to Liverpool. When they dropped the man he said, "I'm going to do you a favour guv. Thanks," and threw the police chief's notebook and wallet through the car window to him.

We spent a lively hour discussing the eccentrics of the last centuries and I remembered that we have a few eccentrics in this century, and proceeded to recall a few I'd known.

Lady Manning was very elegant, renowned for getting drunk, but she never drove the car while drunk. She used to phone the hotel where she lived and I was manageress. One day she swayed up to the reception desk in the late afternoon with a gorgeous black hat.

"Do you like it?" she asked. I assured her that it was a work of art and made her look charming. Her daughter-in-law arrived five minutes later and five minutes after that she stepped out of the lift and banged the hat on my head saying "Keep it, you're a fool. My daughter-in-law said it looks hideous." I was delighted. It had cost the equivalent of my month's salary.

Anne was collecting the cups and putting them on the trolley when she heard Mrs Hart say, "There were more eccentric people round when I was young than now. They were mostly good people who made life more interesting for us dull mortals."

Then Anne babbled out, "Sure, and aren't the best eccentric people in Ireland? Sure, 'tis full of them."

"Quite," said Mr McGregor. We only needed you here with some of your stories to complete the afternoon.

Miss Beam said that she'd written out a miming play to entertain the guests, and could she borrow the fancy dress clothes we kept in the attic? I took the box to her room. I never asked her what the play was about and imagined that she herself would be dolling up in the clothes. Two days later I was amazed. She'd dressed up eight of the guests and, as you can guess, six of them were guests that hadn't any memory. One was standing in the corner, another sitting on the floor, and three of them were wandering aimlessly about. Miss Beam was issuing orders to the others on what to say or do with their hands. A

161

stranger coming into the hall would have thought it was a loony bin, and I could see by the faces of some of them that they were utterly confused.

I apologised and said the clothes were needed, and helped to undress them. I then suggested that she sat them round a table and taught them a card game, which she did. The good padre came to the rescue and advised those who hadn't a clue which card to play.

Jim said later, "You must have been mad not to enquire what it was all about before you gave her the clothes."

I phoned John to ask him to pick up a book I'd ordered in London and bring it with him on Sunday. I said, "Hello, John. How are you? It's me, Lillian." He said, "Hello Lillian." I proceeded to talk about the weather, the new records we'd bought and the books I'd read. He agreed that Beethoven, Brahms and Mozart were unbeatable.

"How's Alison?" I asked. He sounded puzzled.

"Who's Alison?" he said.

"Oh, don't be silly, John. Who's Alison? It's your wife," I said.

"I haven't got a wife," he replied.

We spent a couple of minutes sorting it out. He sounded exactly like our John. He was very gallant, and said he was sorry because he'd thought it was the start of a beautiful friendship!

Jim reminded me of the time that the Major wanted me to book him in at Osborne on the Isle of Wight. When the operator said, "What town?" I had replied, "Cowes". "How dare you!" she said, and hung up. We don't know whether it was my voice or her ignorance of geography. Perhaps she was new.

As you can see there's never a dull moment. Last weekend was funny, and before I say "goodnight" I must tell you what happened.

June came to stay for the weekend. Her son is home from university and has got himself a job until he goes back.

"What is he doing?" I enquired.

"He's a bank messenger," June replied.

"We ought to play a joke on him."

"He'd never fall for it. You'd never catch him," said June.

"Do you want to bet? It's worth a try," I said.

"Very well, you try," she said. I spent a few minutes working it out and then phoned.

"This is Barclays Bank. Have you got your pen handy? This is an emergency," I said, making my voice as deep as I could.

"Yes, Yes," said Charles.

"Take this down. 20 pounds of 22 carat gold, 14 pounds of silver, 55 one carat diamonds. Have you got that?"

"Yes," said Charles.

"I'll put my secretary on to you. Read it back so that we know you've got it down correctly," I said. Jim spoke to him using a different accent.

"Where do I take it to?" asked Charles when Jim finished.

"Home, you bloody fool," said Jim in his own voice. Charles was hysterical and so was his mother.

Home made fun is always the best so I'll say "goodnight".

Look forward to your news.

Much love,
Lillian.

My dear Tilly,

I described the lovely six bedroomed home we've bought (over the phone!) to remove the guests to, in case we lost out at court. It has a dining room and three reception rooms. As you know, we were going to sell it if we won, but now we'll be moving and will not face the worry of maybe going bankrupt through the court case.

We went to London to see Mr Down, the solicitor. He said we should take the compensation and move, and that we could be faced with redecorating inside and out.

"Nonsense. It's all been done in the last 12 months," I said. He said it didn't make any difference, because once a picture was removed from a wall a slightly different shade would appear on the wall, justifying the owner in demanding it was redecorated. We argued for half an hour before returning home.

The next day he phoned to say that they had offered to double the compensation.

"Never," I replied.

One week later he phoned again to enquire if we would accept the last offer being doubled.

"Never," we said.

Another two weeks passed and I was tidying up the top shelves in the office. Some books fell on the floor, and out dropped some papers.

Tilly, what a surprise! They were the papers the local authority had sent 14 years ago, informing Mrs Gilbert that they intended closing the home because she hadn't put in fire precautions, and that they didn't consider a couple with a baby and an aged mother sufficient staff to look after 21 old people. The next day we rushed out to get four copies made — one for our lawyer, one for the doctor, one for ourselves. The fourth, Jim took and handed in to her solicitor's office. I sat and prayed in the car. I've never prayed so hard.

I got back in time to serve the lunch and, five minutes later, the phone rang. It was our solicitor, who said, "They have just rung me to say they wish to double that last offer".

"No, never! I'm not turning the people out. They want to run luxury flats once they are gone. No, they have to sign to keep the people, and they have to buy all the bedroom furniture. I'll give them the dining room and lounge furniture and furnishings, plus the new oil-fired Aga cooker and kitchen equipment, because the old people must be looked after. If they refuse, we go to court." I hung up.

Ten minutes later he phoned back to say that they'd accepted, so now we've packed and repacked and it's all go. We made all the guests' relatives aware of the situation so they would take precautions to see that they were looked after, but the Major left, saying he couldn't possibly stay in the place without us. Four guests are to come with us because they have been with us such a long time, and two of them couldn't afford increases. The relatives decided that they should come with us, and will visit them every couple of months, as we will be so far away.

The solicitor was sharp. He put a bill in for one tenth of the settlement, which is all we'd have got if we'd taken his advice. Jim told him, "My wife won this case, not you," and he reduced his bill!

Two months ago we paid a surveyor's fee of £80 for a five hour survey of the house we've bought. Here, we employed a different surveyor. He came to lunch, spent one and a half hours walking round the building with us, describing as the solicitor had done that they might insist on redecorating if a painting or heavy furniture was moved. His bill was £200. Jim wrote and asked him to explain the differences in the bills. He reduced it by half.

I can see that Jim should have been either a solicitor or a surveyor after this. They have a far easier life, but my praise for barristers is unlimited. They all refused to charge. Isn't that marvellous, Tilly?

The guests who are staying held a cocktail party to wish us good luck, and thank us for looking after them.

If we'd been rich we would have taken the owner to court if necessary, having found the evidence in our favour, but we don't think it would ever have got to the stage of going to court in the circumstances.

One day I might get the time to write about the worries and joys we've had in the last seven years. The joys far exceed the worries, but I would like to pass on our experiences so that other people contemplating running a home for the elderly would benefit from reading about the financial risks, and realise that it is the one field in which one must have love for each individual soul, and a respect to enable them, *compos mentis* or otherwise, to live a happy and dignified existence on this earth.

The staff are staying on, and that will be a comfort to the guests, so now I am off to bed to make an early start tomorrow. The next time you hear from me will be in the New Year.

Meanwhile, I'll phone you on Christmas Eve.

Much love,
Lillian.